Food on a Budget
Family Meals

This is a **FLAME TREE** book
First published in 2009

Publisher and Creative Director: Nick Wells
Project Editor: Cat Emslie
Art Director: Mike Spender
Layout Design: Dave Jones
Digital Design and Production: Chris Herbert
Picture Research: Toria Lyle and Cat Emslie
Proofreader: Dawn Laker
Indexer: Helen Snaith

Special thanks to Megan Mizanty

09 11 13 12 10
1 3 5 7 9 10 8 6 4 2

This edition first published 2009 by
FLAME TREE PUBLISHING
Crabtree Hall, Crabtree Lane
Fulham, London SW6 6TY
United Kingdom

www.flametreepublishing.com

Flame Tree is part of The Foundry Creative Media Co. Ltd
© The Foundry Creative Media Co. Ltd

ISBN 978-1-84786-529-8

A CIP Record for this book is available from the British Library upon request

Printed in India

Notes on currencies and recipes:

Where monetary equivalents are given they are either commensurate (i.e. £1 = US$1) or, where appropriate, the exchange rate of 1.4 dollars to the pound has been applied. The measurements provided in this book are presented as metric/imperial/US cups, using practical equivalents; certain foods and cooking items that are termed differently in the UK and in North America are presented as 'UK term/US term'; and eggs are medium (UK)/large (US), and large (UK)/extra-large (US).

Author's acknowledgements:

Many thanks to my mum, Veronica Girard, for teaching me to cook when I was seven years old.
The various sources used when compiling the information in this book include: US Department of Agriculture; Center for Nutrition Policy and Promotion; UK National Health Service (NHS); UK Office for National Statistics; World Health Organization; *The Metro Recipe Book*, South Metropolitan Gas Company, 1936, courtesy of Beryl Girard (meat paste recipe on page 137); *Apple Pie and the Maple Leaf: 100 Years of Canadian Home Cooking*, unpublished, author's family's own (chocolate cake recipe on page 172 and rock cakes recipe on page 131); *Victory Cookbook: Nostalgic Food and Facts from 1940–1954*, Maguerite Patten OBE in association with the Imperial War Museum, courtesy of Barbara Brine; www.celtnet.org.uk (stuffed heart recipe on page 127); www.storingandfreezing.co.uk; www.fruitexpert.co.uk; and www.lovefoodhatewaste.com. The case studies are based on real families known to the author (names may have been changed to protect identities).

All pictures courtesy of Foundry Arts except the following, which are courtesy of Shutterstock and © the following photographers: 1 & 91 Tiggy Gallery!; 3 & 31 Andrew Horwitz; 4 & 16 Milos Jaric; 5 & 58 Morgan Lane Photography; 6 & 102 Liv friis-larsen; 7(b) & 188 ahlan; 7(t) & 174 Bochkarev Photography; 74(b) Analia Valeria Urani; 74(t), 114 Kheng Guan Toh; 8 & 200, 11, 15, 21, 29, 62, 108, 110, 120, 126, 128, 141, 145, 151, 173 Monkey Business Images; 9(b) & 240 Paul Binet; 9(t) & 220 Alistair Rennie; 10, 25, 123, 148 Losevsky Pavel; 12 Leah-Anne Thompson; 13 Alexey Stiop; 14 wrangler; 18 Provasilich; 19 Brian A Jackson; 22 Lepas; 24, 89 iofoto; 28 jirkaejc; 33 Chepko Danil Vitalevich; 35 Stanislav Crnjak; 37, 82 Elena Elisseeva; 39 Sasha Semenov-Maron; 40 hardtmuth; 42 Marc van Vuren; 43 cen; 45 V. J. Matthew; 46 Carlos Caetano; 49 Jonathan Feinstein; 50, 164 Roman Sigaev; 51, 138 Picsfive; 53 Katrina Brown; 55 Fotaw; 57 Barbro Wickström; 60 Nuno Garuti; 63 Robert Redelowski; 65 Andrea Skjold; 68 Danijel Micka; 69 Antonio Munoz Palomares; 70 hasanugurlu; 72 matka_Wariatka; 76 radarreklama; 77 ivanastar; 78 Robert Anthony; 81 Andrjuss ; 83 Darren K. Fisher; 85 polat ; 87 Milkos ; 93 Richard Peterson; 95 Douglas Freer; 97 Nayashkova Olga; 98 Tobik; 101 Ba Tu; 105 amfoto; 107 Akhilesh; 109 Alexander Shalamov; 113 Edyta Pawlowska; 119 dimitris_k; 121, 129 Joe Gough; 127 Alistair Cotton; 130 osmozist; 132 hfng; 133 Silvia Bogdanski; 134 Demid; 135 sban ; 139 Hannamariah; 140 Zhiltsov Alexandr; 143 M.antonis ; 144 Iv Nikolny; 146 Robyn Mackenzie; 147 Lisa Eastman; 149 Nicholas Piccillo; 150 Anthony Berenyi ; 153 Magdalena Kucova; 154 Stephen Orsillo; 156 Christopher Elwell; 158 Claude Beaubien; 159 Ussr79; 161 nicobatista; 162 Kurt Tutschek; 163 Yurchyks; 168 digitalife; 169 ryasick photography; 171 Jeremy Smith.

Food on a Budget

Family Meals

SIMONEY GIRARD

Series Foreword: Tony Turnbull

**FLAME TREE
PUBLISHING**

Contents

A budget is not about scrimping and saving or cutting out everything that you enjoy: it is about being realistic and working out how to save money consistently while appeasing the tastebuds. Sticking to the list can be difficult, but it is important to think about the food you actually need, rather than buying on impulse. This chapter shows how organizational skills and willpower are crucial! Where can you find the best discounts – and when? Perhaps you can cut the family's food budget by shopping elsewhere, or at a different time of the day. Changing your habits may help you slash your budget. Getting the best prices is only part of the equation: finding food that the whole family can enjoy, getting the right quantities and making sure you stick to your plan are all factors in successful family shopping. And it could be worth 'thinking outside of the trolley' (or shopping cart) – that is, you do not even have to shop to get delicious food – why not grow your own? Get tips on how.

Family Needs

There is a link between low family incomes and high levels of obesity. But low-budget does not need to mean high-fat. This chapter will bust the 'convenience' myth and show that healthier can easily be cheaper. But you must also consider the specific needs of the different members of the family: what are allergies and intolerances – is there a difference between the two? What foods should you avoid if a family member suffers from any allergies? These can be difficult and expensive to cater for, but there are ways to make it easier and cheaper. Cooking for pregnancies, tickling the toddler's tastebuds, learning how to cater for vegetarians or vegans and thinking of family members with diabetic, heart or age-related health problems – these are all important concerns, but they do not prevent you from preparing meals on a budget.

The Family Kitchen

This chapter looks at ways to get the family involved in preparing meals, helping to take the strain off the person who usually does the cooking. Could your family of four eat a two-course meal for just £5 or $5? You could if you knew about using versatile ingredients, how to prepare and cook inexpensive cuts of meat or fantastic fish dishes and make the most of your store-cupboard essentials. It is not easy to keep cooking new things or to buy new ingredients so that every meal is different. But there are many ways to reuse and make the most of existing ingredients. What is more, you can learn to cook your own sauces, gravies, salad dressings and stuffings out of tiny scraps, which can lead to big savings without wastage. How do you keep food out of the reach of closet snackers? There are many ways to store food to avoid light-fingered nibblers, cut down on the amount of food thrown away and keep food for a long time. Special occasions require your household food budget to go that little bit further. This chapter provides some hints and tips to help it stretch without breaking.

Soups & Starters 174

Soup is one of the most budget-friendly dishes to prepare, while being filling, tasty and nutritious. This chapter has some great recipe suggestions for a refreshing Carrot and Ginger Soup or a delectable Creamy Chicken and Tofu Soup. There are also some inspiring ideas for appetizers – why not tempt the family with some exciting Swedish Cocktail Meatballs or classic Prawn Toasts? All these recipes use ingredients (or suggest alternatives) that should not break the bank, while employing invaluable store-cupboard seasonings and sauces to create delicious flavours.

Fish & Seafood 188

Fish can often be expensive, but earlier on in the book you will have discovered that there is no need to cut back on such a nutritious and tasty component of your diet – it is all about using cheaper cuts, cheaper alternatives to the popular fish and interesting cooking methods – and do not forget the invaluable canned fish. This section offers a recipe for that favourite, cod, but also for all sorts of casseroles and bakes that could use a myriad of fish – from Chunky Halibut Casserole and Fish Crumble to lip-smacking Tuna Cannelloni. Do not forget those smaller fish, which can prove to be exquisite eaten fresh – try our Sardines with Redcurrants.

Meat & Poultry 200

Some would expect meat to be the first thing cut out of the diet when cooking on a budget, but this is ridiculous. Just as with fish, as long as you are cunning about what, where and when you buy, you can create all sorts of tasty meat dishes. Again, why not exploit those less popular cuts of meat? These can be used to create the juiciest, richest, most melt-in-the-mouth morsels in stews and casseroles, such as the family favourite, Steak and Kidney Stew. We must not forget the invaluable and versatile minced/ground meat – a staple ingredient when cooking on a budget, whether it be beef, lamb, pork, chicken or turkey – try our

Spaghetti Bolognese, Lamb and Potato Moussaka or Turkey and Mixed Mushroom Lasagne. Importantly, we have included a recipe for Slow Roast Chicken with Potatoes and Oregano as a family's diet would be incomplete without a Sunday roast, not least because cooking a whole chicken can contribute to more than one meal and thus really be worth the cost.

Vegetables 220

Vegetables are the stars of the budget kitchen. Not only are they cheaper than meat and fish, but they excel in nutrition, variety and taste. Buy in season and you will make even more savings, not to mention reduce your carbon footprint by not buying vegetables flown halfway around the world. And, of course, you could even cook with vegetables you have grown yourself! This chapter suggests a whole range of tantalizing vegetable stews, curries, salads, pasta and rice dishes and pies, influenced by flavours from around the world. For example, enjoy a classic Vegetarian Spaghetti Bolognese, a hearty Roasted Vegetable Pie, indulgent Pumpkin-filled Pasta with Butter and Sage or a tasty Creamy Chickpea Curry.

Desserts & Sweet Treats

During these credit-crunched times, the last thing you want to do is cut out all treats – and you do not have to. Families deserve something a little sweet now and then, while still maintaining a healthy diet that is not loaded with sugar and fat. This selection provides a range of desserts

and treats, from the fruity to the more indulgent, whose simple ingredients mean none of them should stretch the wallet too far. Try a traditional, creamy Rice Pudding or the more virtuous Oaty Fruit Puddings, luxuriate in the Rich Double-crust Plum Pie or please the kids with a Frozen Mississippi Mud Pie, or munch on some delectable Chocolate Chip Cookies.

Series Foreword

Last night I made a chorizo and chickpea casserole. I sweated some onions in a little olive oil, threw in the chopped-up Spanish sausage and, once it had released its golden, paprika-spiked juices, I added chicken stock, chickpeas and some sliced cabbage. It bubbled away happily for about twenty minutes, and then I finished it off with a squeeze of lemon juice and a bit of seasoning and ate it with a crust of bread. It probably cost a total of three pounds and was utterly delicious, even if I do say so myself.

Did I do it to be cheap? Not at all – although the fact that it didn't break the bank was certainly a bonus. I did it because that is what proper cooking is about – taking a few raw ingredients and, through the alchemy of heat, creating a dish that is greater than the sum of its parts.

People get too hung up on price anyway. Budget cooking doesn't necessarily mean cheap cooking. It doesn't mean filling your fridge with two-for-ones or limp vegetables going cheap at the market. It's more a state of mind, of being aware of what food is costing you and making the most of what you then buy. Sometimes I like to cook a beautiful steak or a whole sea bass, neither of which can be called cheap, but if I can wring maximum value out of them, it's money well spent.

Let's go back to that chorizo casserole. The most expensive element was the chorizo. I got mine from my local butcher so, while it wasn't authentically Spanish, it was half the price. I wouldn't serve it thinly sliced with an aperitif, but for throwing into a stew it was well up to the job. Why pay extra if you aren't going to appreciate its nuances of flavour? Ditto the olive oil – only a fool fries with extra virgin – save that for dressing a salad or finished dish.

The stock was home-made, using the carcass from a Sunday roast, plus the peelings from the leeks and carrots I served it with. That doesn't mean it was free, because, to make a decent stock, you need to start with a decent, free-range chicken. But it meant I could justify buying the more expensive bird and enjoying its superior flavour, because I knew it would be giving me not one, but two meals.

So, spend your money where it counts, and plan ahead. These are the cornerstones of budget cooking. It's not about deprivation, but about that rather old-fashioned notion of good housekeeping. And finally, don't beat yourself up too much. I ended up using two cans of instant chickpeas, when I should really have soaked my own the night before. But really, pre-soaking chickpeas? Who's got time for that?

Tony Turnbull is food and drink editor of *The Times*

Introduction

Shopping, planning and cooking for your family on a tight budget is becoming harder for millions of people. We have seen a massive global credit crunch, rising inflation, a reduction in lending and a squeeze on our spending and saving.

For example, the World Bank said that, in April 2008, food prices globally had risen 40 per cent year on year and 83 per cent over three years. You just have to compare the price of your shopping bills to prove this. According to the UK's Office for National Statistics, based on an internationally-agreed classification system (the Classification of Individual Consumption by Purpose), an average household of two adults and two children spend an average £690 ($970) a week on household bills. Transport, housing and energy prove to be the greatest expenses, but fourth on the list of big-ticket items was food and non-alcoholic drink. Feeding the family can take a huge chunk out of your income – something that becomes ever more worrying as we read of bonus freezes and the very real threat of redundancy to many people. It is clear that families need all the help they can get to shop within the household budget without restricting them to a limited, boring or unhealthy diet.

Lessons from History

However, thankfully, we are not in unfamiliar territory. There are millions of people alive today around the world who lived through the Great Depression, the Second World War and the post-war gloom. They too had large families to feed, bills to pay and a tight budget on which to live. And they did survive, showing great resourcefulness in the way they shopped, grew their own, cooked and stored their food.

We might, like the war generation, be living in an age where money is tight, lending is greatly curtailed and our bank balances are bleak. However, we do not have to face the same sort of problems of supply: we are blessed with a plethora of shops stocking every type of food under the sun. We neither have strict rations on essential food items, nor do we need to wait until summertime to get strawberries, nor linger until autumn for parsnips. And, unlike the generations of yesteryear, nearly everyone has a freezer, or fridge-freezer at the very least, so we can store food up for a longer time than our forebears.

Food on a Budget Today

Taking these essential differences into account, this book is not advocating a return to the 1940s, to a time of powdered eggs, reusing old teabags and borrowing a cup of sugar from your neighbour. Neither is this about 'digging for victory', nor a moral volume telling you to 'grin and bear it'. But what we are advocating is considering the resourcefulness of our forebears, how they made the most of the little they had, and looking at ways to apply some of these handy hints and tips to our own individual situations.

For example, with a bit of practice, families need never buy any more stocks or soups, pastes or preserves because they can grow, cook, prepare and store them themselves. Even 50 years ago, it was considered a luxury to buy your soups or preserves. Recipes dredged up from the inter-war years and the Second World War celebrations show just how easy it really is to cook some of these things from scratch.

From the Internet back to the Ancients

There are modern ways to make savings, too. The internet has brought with it a host of opportunity at our fingertips: the ability to compare and contrast prices and discounts on offer at various supermarkets; information on how to grow and store our own fresh produce; and useful ideas to help us save electricity and gas when cooking the family meal, for example.

But we do not need to look at the technological wonders of today or the chin-up cookery books of 1940: we can also learn from the ancients about how to cook certain meat dishes that are inexpensive to buy and put together, or how to make slow cookers out of palm leaves, hay, wood and glass. Traditional methods of storing and saving, using and re-using, making do and mending – all these can be applied to today's families having to cope with today's recessionary times.

Changing Mindsets

In addition to learning about the *practicalities* from our forbears, we can also take our cue from them regarding our *attitudes*. When did we get so materialistic? Was it when shops gave way to the big superstores with their cornucopia of foodstuffs? Or was it when we all started to lead such busy, stressful lives that family living went out of the window and we became strangers in our own homes, not eating together, not shopping together, but buying convenience food or takeaways to eat on our own? When did we stop making do and mending? Who rejuvenates faded blouses and tops by dying them another colour? Who fixes their own shoes? These questions might sound strange, but they are the fundamental basis for the mess we are in today. Let's call it 'instantism'. We want it all: instant coffee, instant decisions, instant credit. And what happens when the very system supplying that instant credit goes? Suddenly our decisions become centred around affordability or job-related issues. Suddenly we are looking at the price we pay for a single tall skinny latte in the morning and spending the same amount on a large jar of instant coffee instead.

And it is in this new-found realism about what we really can afford (not what we can borrow) that we also find the cure to 'instantism': long-term perspective about the things that really matter – the people around us in the home where we live. Thinking about what we can do today to help us tomorrow brings with it a new responsibility: planning meals, setting a budget, making lists, considering where we can shop, being thoughtful about how we can best cater for our loved ones and their special dietary and health needs.

Quality on a Budget

So, there is no need to restrict your family to low-cost, high-fat convenience food. Throw the ready meals out of the window and say hello to home-made meals that the whole household will enjoy. They do not have to be fancy, they do not have to be big – but they are clever meals, meals that take into account various dietary requirements, health-related issues and constraints on time – not to mention keeping well within your own family's budget.

Taking all these ingredients, mixing them together with a pinch of common sense, a dash of trial-and-error and equal parts of enthusiasm and dedication, we can feed our families on what seems to be an ever-tightening household spend. And, what is more, we can do it with style. Let this book be a motivation to stop worrying about where the money will come from, and start making great plans to provide good meals for your family the best you can, no matter how tight the budget becomes.

Shopping
for
Families

PACKED WITH
MONEY
SAVING
IDEAS & TIPS

Setting the Budget

The first thing you might say if someone asks you to define 'budget', is: 'a way to save money'. This is a good answer, but it is not completely accurate. 'To budget' can convey the impression that a person has to cut back drastically on the spend. This mentality means that families set unrealistic targets, which can cause further monetary problems. Let us consider what a budget really is and how you can set an achievable goal for your food spend.

Defining a Budget

The economic definition of a budget is: 'a description of a financial plan ... a list of estimates of revenues to, and expenditures by, an agent for a stated period of time. Normally a budget describes a period in the future not the past.' Put into plain English (something which economists are not very good at doing), this reads: 'a budget is a plan where you try to predict how much you will have to spend and how much you are going to spend at a certain time.'

Myths

There are some unhelpful myths, which have put many people off making a budget. A budget is *not* about:

 sitting down and crossing out all the treats you enjoy

 simply doing things on the cheap

Reality

A budget is about:

 being *honest* about what you *can* spend
 being *realistic* about what you are *going* to spend

How Much Can you Spend?

Obviously this depends on your income, and how much is left over after paying off all those other family bills: heating, energy, travel, mortgage, healthcare bills and school fees. Official research statistics prove that families are finding it increasingly difficult to meet food costs: you are not alone if you are wondering how to make ends meet. But even assuming that there is a little left in the barrel after the mortgage and other bills are paid, you also have to be realistic about how much your family shop comes to. How can you gauge what is essential expenditure?

Keep Your Till Receipts

By keeping till receipts, families can look back at, say, three months' worth of receipts and work out what the average spend should be. This can be important in setting your food budget for the year ahead. Here are some benefits of doing this:

 Price rises: You can see which foodstuffs have risen in price. This will help you decide whether a different store might work out to be better value.

✔ **Not-so-little extras**: You can see how much 'extra' and unplanned food items cost. This will help you stick to your shopping list (see 'Planning Ahead', page 25) and avoid shelling out for items you did not consider in the budget plan.

✔ **What do you not eat?** Looking at the receipts, are there any food items you buy that your family does not really eat? Have you just got into the habit of buying six cartons of milk a week, when in fact you only really need four?

✔ **The average spend**: Shopping bills can help you work out an average spend and can help you think about keeping within a certain band. By cutting out the unnecessary and the unplanned, you could set a reasonable budget, setting an upper and lower limit for flexibility, for each week's spend. You will save money immediately if you stick within that band.

✔ **Checking supermarkets**: Comparing receipts from different stores will indicate where to shop for the best prices on your family staples such as cereal, bread, juice and meat. It is not just comparing random prices across each store to see who has got the highest number of discounts, but looking at what your family actually buys and whether this research can help lower your budget.

Think Ahead for Special Occasions

If you know you have a family birthday or celebration coming up, make sure you factor this extra expenditure into your budget. Either set up a separate cash account way in advance to save for this expenditure, or make a sensible budget plan for that week's food spend.

Spend As Much As Your Family Eats

No more, no less! Do not cut back so much that your family meals are insufficient. But do not over-estimate what your family can eat. A filling, healthy meal can be provided within a sensible budget plan.

Case Study: The Family of Three

Rupinder Ford and her husband Michael try to set a budget, but even with just one young son (Ritchie, aged 6), this can be difficult. Rupinder says, 'I do try to set a budget, although with only one child, I am more extravagant than if I had a family of four children. I spend an average of US$100–140 (£70–100) a week, which includes the household cleaning and laundry items as well. The food component is probably $80–100 (£60–70) per week. I stick to my budget 80 per cent of the time, but the other 20 per cent is those luxury extras – I know, it's a lapse!

'I balance my shopping between discount superstores and more luxury-brand food when I want that extra bit of quality. To balance the cost per person, per meal, I tend to cook a lot of pasta or chilli con carne during the week, which works out cheaper, but we have a roast meal on a Sunday. Roasts can be more expensive, but not prohibitively so.

'I do always buy fresh fruit for my young son, who is still on a limited main meal diet. The constraints on him eating are not financial, but are in trying to get him to try new things. But I am increasingly watching what I spend overall, despite having only one child.'

Waste Not, Want Not

If you over-estimate the spend, you will be tempted to use up the full amount, probably on over-priced snack foods or stuff that will only get thrown away. Even in 2008, according to the World Food Programme, consumers in the US, UK and Western Europe were wasting 30 per cent of food purchased. In the US alone, this was worth an estimated US$48.3bn.

Ways Not to Waste

Thinking about what tends to get wasted in your household will help you work out what to buy and what not to buy. Here are some things to help you get started:

- **Forgotten fridge items:** What tends to get left in the fridge until it has curdled its way past its use-by-date? Yoghurts? Pickles? Cut back on buying it.

- **Timing is everything:** Does your family tend to eat more at lunchtime and only want a little to eat in the evening? Then do not buy loads of ingredients for big evening meals, as these are likely to linger until they are thrown out.

- **Only buy what you want:** Buying more than you need means too much waste food at the end of the week.

- **Bake it, don't fake it:** Do you buy several cakes (on the insistence of your eight-year-old) that only get half-eaten? Why not just buy the bare ingredients for baking a cake? It will save money in the long term and provide something fun to do together as a family. (*See* chapter three, The Family Kitchen, page 102.)

Weekly or Monthly Budget?

Those who get paid weekly, or who do not own a car, may find that a smaller, weekly shop is better. In this case, work out how much you can set aside each week for spending, and apportion some of that to the food shop. There are two advantages of weekly shopping:

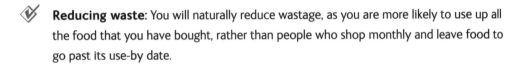 **Reducing waste:** You will naturally reduce wastage, as you are more likely to use up all the food that you have bought, rather than people who shop monthly and leave food to go past its use-by date.

Cash is king: Weekly shoppers may be more likely to use cash to pay for their groceries, so this keeps them within their set budget; it is easy to go overboard when you are carrying around a credit or debit card.

Card Caution

If you shop monthly, you are less likely to carry around a significant wad of cash in your wallet and are more likely to pay by card. This can be risky. Make sure that you are not tempted to bust your budget because you have the 'freedom' to do so on your credit or debit card. By the same token, avoid buying too much food that will only get wasted simply because you can. In both instances, the point is to stick within a reasonable, achievable budget and to see where you can shave off unnecessary expenses.

Where Do Your Priorities Lie?

It may be very difficult for you to make a regular budget. Perhaps you are self-employed or working on a contract-only basis, or you have debt problems. If there is only a certain amount left in the kitty and your average monthly shop is at least four times that amount, you either try to make do on what you have (which might be an unrealistic expectation, considering the number of people in the family) or you sort out what other expenditures you have been laying out that require attention. You have to eat to live.

Ask Yourself How to Prioritize

By taking time to go through your finances at the start of the month, you will find you can set aside the right amount to cover important costs, such as the family food budget, without getting further into debt or cutting back so far that you end up with beans for supper every night.

- **Eat out less:** Perhaps you could go out less and put more food on the table?

- **Rearrange or pay off your loans:** Do you need to sort out your loan arrangements so that you do not have to shell out such high rates of interest on repayments?

Who Can Help with Financial Planning?

In these recessionary times, it is important to get some specialist advice to help out if you are really struggling. Possible sources of help are:

- **Bank:** A personal representative at your bank should be able to give you some free budgeting advice.

- **Independent financial adviser:** If you pay a fee, as opposed to commission, you should get completely impartial advice on your situation. The internet offers various ways of searching for a qualified adviser in your area.

- **Your accountant:** If you have your own accountant, make use of them!

- **A debt specialist:** You can contact a debt specialist at a free, charity-based service such as Mind or the Citizens Advice Bureau in the UK, or the Credit Council of America.

Planning Ahead

So, you have your budget sorted out and whether you tend to shop monthly or weekly. Now it comes to planning ahead. This is the best way to save money and stick within your budget – and it really takes no time at all! We are not talking about a military-style operation towards family meals, but taking a couple of minutes to think ahead about what you need could save you a lot of money.

Making a List

Making a list sounds like something your granny does for a hobby, but it is really important. How many times have you come back from the supermarket without the toilet rolls or washing-up liquid? How many times have you, instead, bought six or seven items that you did not need, just because you were not sure whether you needed them or not?

Helping Children to Understand the List

Parents will know that it can be effective for younger children if you explain beforehand about the list. They can understand that the list is law and it is a good example to set them.

Bear in mind, however, that you should apply the same rule to yourselves as adults in the interests of a) fairness, b) setting a good example and c) sticking to your budget.

Compiling Tips

Instead of rushing at the last minute to make a list of things you need to get, or not bothering at all and picking up anything you see, try the following:

The till receipts: Use your last few shopping bills as a basis for remembering certain items and working out which supermarkets could offer the best price on your family essentials.

Who ate the last cookie (and left the pack on the side)? Take note of 'empties' during the week. Why not keep a magnetic notepad on the fridge and train yourself (and your family) to write down when they finish an item? This might help you even more if you have the sort of family that leaves empty tubs in the fridge for you to find after you come back from the shop.

Running on empty: Make a note of everyday items that are running low, especially those items which might not be as widely available in many supermarkets. These might be things such as special soya milk or gluten-free bread, if you or a member of your family has certain intolerances or allergies (*see* chapter two, Family Needs, page 58).

Keep the coupons handy: If you have particular money-off coupons, or have saved up loyalty points or stamps, make sure that you keep these with the list, in your wallet or purse, ready for the big shop.

Branded for Life

How many times have you or a family member bought the wrong brand or flavour of something, only for it to sit on the shelf until it gets thrown away? Keeping a list can also help you remember which brand and type of food went down well with the family, and which brands were met with general disapproval. This will help reduce unnecessary spending and keep your household budget low.

Planning the Weekly Meals

If you have a rough plan in your head for what the week has in store in terms of meals, you will be able to include the appropriate components in your list. This has several advantages:

✅ **You will have what you need**: You will not have to rush out last-minute to a more expensive local or convenience store.

✅ **Versatility**: You can think about what ingredients you might buy that can be used in several ways.

✅ **Precision**: You can gauge quantities more precisely, so you do not end up buying more than you need.

✅ **Special needs**: Any family members with particular likes or dislikes, allergies or intolerances can be catered for well in advance.

✅ **Destination planning**: You can figure out where to go for the best deals on certain food items you need for various meals.

✅ **Cooking for more**: If you are going to have someone over for dinner one night, you can think ahead to make the most of any bargains or bulk buy discounts.

A List is for Life, Not Just for January

Many people start to make a list but either do not keep it or forget items. Here is what shoppers from around the world do:

✅ **James Aaron, Dubai, UAE**: 'I always make a list as I have a bad memory. Also, if I shop when I'm hungry, I only tend to get things for that evening, so have to go shopping again in the week.'

✅ **Elenora Chen, New York, US**: 'I tend to buy stuff that doesn't perish, such as tinned tomatoes and dried pasta. I just keep these topped up like a war cupboard! If I want anything exciting I go out and eat. As I tend to buy the same stuff, I can always remember what I'm low on.'

Antony Bleake, South Africa: 'I make a list when I go wine shopping but not food shopping, as I work very near a large supermarket and there is no real need to stockpile food. Wine, on the other hand ...'

Daphne Wayne-Bough, Belgium: 'I always make a list when I go for a big food shop. However, I often leave it at home.'

Susan Simon, Melbourne, Australia: 'I don't make lists but my boyfriend does! I like to mosey through, seeing what's new, and he likes to get in and out of the shop as quickly as possible and always sticks to his list. I don't worry about what I buy but I always tend to get the cheapest staples (beans, etc) and don't like to pay over a few bucks for anything.'

DeeDee Udele, Surrey, England: 'Seventy-five per cent of the time I don't make a list but, when I do, I stick to it. Sometimes, I miss things off the list that I only remember when I get to the shop. I then handwrite it in at the bottom.'

Irene Manning, London, England: 'I nearly always stick to my list and tend to jot things down when I think of them during the week. But sometimes I get a little tempted, although I try to take just cash with me to prevent me from overspending. The temptation is there, but I have the list, my cash and I rarely go beyond it.'

Forging New Habits

Creating and sticking to your budget parameters, planning your weekly shop and writing a list sound like a drag but they are invaluable good habits to get into. Received wisdom suggests that it takes 21 days to form a habit, but only seven days to break it. So make your budget, list and forward planning habits that stick. They will give you a great start in your quest to cut your shopping spend down immediately, and keep it down throughout the year.

When to Shop

We all lead busy lives, and it is no wonder that the majority of us pile down to the nearest supermarket on a Saturday or Sunday in order to get in the weekly or monthly groceries. But this can lead to a quick-dash in crowded supermarkets, fractious children and hungry teenagers loitering wistfully around the freshly-baked cookies counter. Being stressed leads to the famous phrase: 'Let's just get out of here as quickly as possible', which can lead to picking up the first thing you see, rather than having the leisure to compare prices or search for the best bargains.

The Early Bird Catches the Worm

Why not get up a little earlier and shop when there are fewer people around and a clearer car park? You will have more leisure to follow your list and pick up more bargains along the way.

Evening Advantages

Or, if you can shop later on in the evening, and especially on a weekday, you will not only find that it is not so crowded and you have the time to think about what you are buying but you will also find that many supermarkets do discounts on big-ticket items towards the end of the day. And individual stores will set their own end-of-line bargain prices, which you will not see if you go online to compare superstores.

End-of-day Discounts

Items that are often discounted in large chains include:

- **Freshly-baked produce**: bread, bagels, croissants, cakes. These are still good for a few days afterwards, but shelves need to be cleared for the next day's batch.

- **Milk or dairy produce**: If you are going to eat yoghurts, use up the cheese or drink the milk within a day or two of the use-by date, then it is fine to buy them. You can also store the milk in the freezer to prolong its life.

- **End-of-line or special offers**: Sometimes, foodstuffs such as cereal may have had a 50-per-cent-free offer which is coming to an end.

- **Fresh fruit and vegetables**: Obviously these have a short shelf life so need to be turned around fairly quickly.

End-of-day Discount Don'ts

Things to watch out for on discounted items include:

- **Meat on the turn**: If meat looks grey or has a greenish tinge, do not buy it, even if it is cheap. It is also off.

- **Bulging cans and cartons**: Check that tinned food is not bulging outwards. An inward dent is fine, but if it is bulging outwards, it means the food inside is spoiled. If juice cartons are bulging, then they are fermenting and have gone off.

- **Cheap does not mean necessary**: Do not be misled into thinking that because it is a 'bargain', you must need it. If it is not on the list, do not buy it.

Where to Shop?

In a busy world where we are cash-strapped and time-poor, it is difficult to make the right choices about where to shop. The local convenience store may be close and open all hours, but probably costs significantly more than the supermarket that is 20 minutes' drive away. However, for some families, if they do not have a car, or if there is just one parent, who has to work, the convenience store can be the easiest and default option. But how do you tell who has the best bargains?

Advertising

TV, radio and other advertising will promote certain deals on various goods to lure you into the big-name stores. But remember that no one is offering you anything without a catch – the stores need your custom and they will get money out of you. Here are a few pointers to get you started:

Do Not Get Carried Away!

Take advantage of stores that are advertising discounts on items you usually buy. But do not get carried away by the big signs and special offer labels placed at eye-catching intervals.

Leaflets and Promotions

Make the most of any that come through your door. These will give you a good indication of which shops are in a price war on certain items, or which supermarket is having a super sale on. If there are any vouchers on items that you need, take these with you.

Warnings Apply

Leaflets and promotions are another way of hooking you. So take the flyer with you, but look around.

Shop Around

You do not have to visit several stores before you decide which ones have the best price. But do keep an open mind as to which shop might be better value for you, rather than just listening to the adverts.

Keep the Receipts

As mentioned before, comparing these in the comfort of your own home will help you work out where to go for the best deals for your family.

Online Shopping

The world is changing fast: we are not living in 1948, where shops shut at 5 p.m., never opened on a Sunday and all stocked exactly the same items. Nowadays, stores stock a wide variety of foodstuffs from all over the world, are open seven days a week and some are open all hours. But they are also recognizing that many people do not have the ability or time to do big weekly or monthly shops in store. Many supermarkets now offer online shopping, complete with door-to-door delivery, which can benefit you if you:

 are unable to get to the shops physically
 do not have the time to go
 are likely to spend as much on petrol as on delivery

User-friendly

Busy mother-of-two Misha Sergeant, Leicester, UK, says, 'When I'm just not able to get out to the shops, I find that internet shopping is quite a good way of making sure you only get what you need. As you look at the various items in your virtual basket, you can review the list and add on anything you have forgotten. Also, I have often got up, looked in my fridge and cupboards to see what I need, then gone back to the computer and added these to the basket ... and taken away things I didn't really need.'

Ask If There Are Any Discounts

Many of these delivery sites will have special delivery discounts and concessions for those who are elderly or have a disability, while others will offer 'extras' to boost online ordering.

Price Comparison on the Internet

A quick search for 'best prices for food shopping' will throw up a host of comparison websites, useful chat forums and even blogs that can help you compare prices. Some websites have updates to let you know which stores have recently discounted certain ranges and which stores are offering the best prices on certain foodstuffs, so you can get a pretty good picture of where you might be able to save money. Some sites claim that you can save between 20 and 30 per cent on your average family food shop. So, even if you do not intend to *buy* online, the internet can help you save money on your shop.

Price Comparison Websites

There are some websites that enable you to automatically compare specific food prices in competing superstores. Two examples are www.mysupermarket.co.uk (for the whole of the UK) or www.lowpricereport.ca (for Ontario). This is how some food shopping price comparison websites work, all the way through to purchasing your shop:

 'Shop': Pick a supermarket and fill your virtual trolley with your usual range of shopping.

 Swap: Conduct a shopping trolley swap with another supermarket – this takes about 60 seconds, depending on how much is in your virtual trolley.

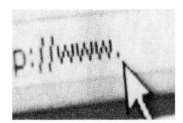

See: See how much you could save by the swap – it could be as much as 20–30 per cent each week.

 Order: Choose which supermarket you will buy from and you will be transferred to that shop's website in order to place your order, ready for it to be delivered to you.

Earn Points

Some price comparison sites have a loyalty scheme where you can gain virtual points with them as well as the usual points you will get with your specific supermarket and on your store loyalty or club card. These virtual points can be traded at other sites for a variety of goods, days out or gifts.

Find the Best Prices

Some websites will show daily deals and best prices on a range of products at each supermarket. So, regardless of whether you want to swap supermarkets or not, you can see at a glance where the best prices are.

Deals of the Week

Each supermarket will feature its latest deals on its own website, whether weekly or daily. It is worth taking a peek at your store's website before you go shopping; if you have time, look at the nearest rival's website too, to see just what is on offer.

Discount Stores

The well-established brand name superstores are facing stiff – and increasingly public – competition from non-domestic, self-proclaimed 'hypermarkets' such as Aldi, Lidl and Netto. Offering significant discounts to the big name rivals, these are springing up all over the UK and starting to make inroads into North America. While other food giants are cutting jobs and closing stores, these newer discount stores are growing in popularity.

How Can They Do It?

There are many ways that these stores make money. These are just a few reasons the stores can sell food cheaply:

- **Bulk-buying**: These stores work on the bulk-buy rule – they place a certain number of orders for crates of food from suppliers, but cannot always guarantee what they are going to get.

- **Tax advantages**: Because they are foreign companies, and their suppliers are often based overseas, they can pass on to customers any VAT advantages accruing to them by law.

- **Low overheads**: The stores are low-budget and do not look fancy. If you want nice shopping centres, shops with polished floors and beautiful layouts, then this overhead and expenditure will be factored into the price you pay for your shopping.

- **No free bags**: If you do not come with your own bags, you will have to pay for their plastic bags at the counter – another way they can keep food prices low.

- **Fast and furious**: These stores do not pay for additional staff to monitor the aisles or pack your bags for you. You have to pack them yourself – and quickly. The stores work on volume of people 'processed' at the tills and will not like it if you hold the line up.

- **Close to the end**: Look at the use-by dates on the food packets ... some of them may be nearing the cut-off point.

Temptation: These stores work on the law of temptation, hoping that you will forget the list when you see how many great buys there are. In this way, the organized family hunt for a good deal becomes a lure to break the budget on unnecessary 'eye candy.' Some of their more expensive food items such as wines and cakes are put right alongside the counter – and when you are waiting in the long queues, this is a great temptation.

Are They Really Always Cheaper?

There are many surveys online which can help to gauge whether or not these stores really do offer better value for money. This is based not just on the number of food items sold at a lower price, but also the quality and the quantity (for example, whether the bulk buys offer a better saving in a cheaper outlet than a no-name or own-brand bulk buy in a 'domestic' store). A simple Google search will throw up some of these websites.

Which Foods Are Cheaper in These Stores?

The answer may be 'pretty much everything'. Food that is generally cheaper than in a standard supermarket includes:

- meat
- cheese (significantly so)
- bulk-buy pastas, noodles, rice
- loose vegetables (check the freshness, though)
- snack foods and party mix
- frozen 'finger food' for parties
- traditional Christmas or holiday 'fayre'
- cartons of fruit juice
- cans of fruit or pie and pastry filling
- four- and six-pack cans of soup, beans, pasta shapes (half the price)

Open Your Mind

Do not be put off by the fact that labels may be primarily in Spanish, German or Polish – most have translations into English. Many of these discounted items are leading brands in Mexico, Germany or Spain, similar to the leading brands in 'domestic' stores. Do not assume that it cannot be any good because it is an unfamiliar brand. You may find that it tastes better and is even healthier.

Taste-tester

One mother who has changed her shopping habits recently, writes, 'When I'm being really organized, I have a computer spreadsheet with the various prices, depending on where I'm shopping. I do most of my food shopping at the new foreign outlet stores. This is not just due to the crunch, but because of the quality of food I can find at a reasonable price.'

The Farmers' Market

These are more popular in rural England and the more countrified areas of the US and Canada, but are starting to make inroads into the cities thanks to the rising popularity of organic and free-range food. Markets are sometimes bypassed in this busy age of instant consumerism, but the experience is great, not to mention the potential for best-price bargains on fresh and home-made food. With a little careful planning, you can find out where the local markets are each week or month, and perhaps going to a farmers' market might become a nice day out for the family once a month.

What Can You Get?

Although you cannot get a lot of the items you may buy in bulk from the supermarkets, such as cans and other non-perishables, there is still a wide range of produce available from farmers' markets (not to mention non-food items such as crafts):

- ✔ fresh meat and meat produce
- ✔ cheeses
- ✔ sauces, pickles, syrups and jams
- ✔ home-made wines and cordials
- ✔ bread, cakes and pastries
- ✔ home-grown vegetables and fruit
- ✔ creams, butters and other dairy produce

Are They Cheaper?

A farmers' market is not always cheaper. But the advantages are that they offer:

- ✔ different choice of produce to supermarkets
- ✔ trustworthy free-range and organic meat
- ✔ food without preservatives or 'hidden nasties'
- ✔ improved taste – especially fruit and vegetables
- ✔ a way to support local farmers and smallholdings
- ✔ an experience – often with live music and family entertainment

How to Save at a Farmers' Market

There are some cost-savings to be had at farmers' markets, however:

- ✔ **Organic savings**: Superstores usually charge higher fees on organic meat than you would pay for the same quality at a farmers' market.

- ✔ **Try before you buy**: You can taste before you buy, which means that if you do not like it, you do not have to buy it, unlike a supermarket where you have to buy first and thus risk wasting food.

- ✔ **Negotiation**: Many of the farmers will do deals or haggle a price with you for bulk buys, so do not go by price tags alone.

The Traditional Market

Because many of these stallholders will import their food directly, they are not subject to the same tax restrictions as the supermarkets are. Plus, they want to sell off their goods at the end of the day because they do not have the storage – so competing cheaply on volume is the way to do it. Finally, the overheads a market trader will have to pay are very low compared with the bills a store has to face.

Different Tastes

Immigration has done a wonderful thing in injecting new life into the flagging marketplaces of cities. It has brought new tastes and food ideas to the fore and has found a willing audience of people wanting to try new things without having to pay the higher prices that a supermarket will front-load on to the goods.

Cheeses, Wines and Olives

Markets will often have specialist French, Greek or Italian stalls selling authentic fresh cheese, wine and produce such as olives at very low prices – and for larger amounts than you would get in a superstore.

Chillies and Chutneys

You can buy spices and herbs in bulk in many markets – something that is just not possible in a superstore. Buying a large bag of, say, paprika or chilli powder means you probably will not have to buy another one for up to 18 months. This can be purchased at the market stall for only a little more than you would pay for a tiny packet of similar herbs and spices at your superstore – and lasts a great deal longer.

Fruit and Veg

There are several advantages at markets when it comes to fruit and vegetables:

- **By weight, not unit:** Because market stalls charge according to weight, you will save money by getting just the right portions you want, without wasting any.

- **Exotic competition:** Some exotic fruit, such as mangoes, pineapples, yams and plantains are far cheaper in markets or local grocery stores than in supermarkets.

- **You do not pay for packaging:** Try this challenge – buy a packet of tomatoes from a supermarket and the same number of fresh ones loose from a market stall. The market stall's local produce will usually work out to be the best price for (usually) fresher goods.

- **Organic food:** You will not pay supermarket prices for buying fresh, home-grown, organic produce from a local marketplace.

Fishmongers and Butchers

Sometimes it is best to cut out the middleman and go straight to the wholesalers. Superstores do not offer you the full range of meat cuts or always show you the best fish dishes to fit your family budget. Many people wrongly assume that a butcher or fishmonger is going to be more expensive as you pay a premium for the freshest meat, or that, because he is a smallholding, his higher overheads will be passed on to you. However, you could save a significant amount by learning how to cook some of the less usual cuts available at butchers and also learn how to make your family meals more varied, healthy and exciting.

Direct from Source

Getting to buy fresh fish directly from the wharf means you will buy them at wholesale prices, rather than retail prices. You can buy in bulk and then freeze and store them, knowing you have the freshest fish possible. It is not always possible to buy direct from the meat farmer but if you can, you will also be able to pay wholesale, not retail, prices.

A Meaty Difference

While supermarket-bought meat is convenient and cleanly-packed, there are certain things to watch out for with meat in supermarkets:

- **The 'water' load:** Many shops will inject water into meat to help it freeze. So when they weigh meat, some stores will not take into account the water load and will charge you for both the meat and the water therein. The water, of course, evaporates in the cooking process, meaning you actually got less for your money.

- **Actual weight v. price:** Also, while on the subject of weight, bear in mind that many weight-based prices fluctuate significantly on products such as cheese or meat, but the actual difference in terms of what you get to serve up on your plate is not always as great as the price may lead you to believe. For example, eight lamb chops might vary 'by weight' by as much as 50p ($1). But will that variation make a difference to what your family will eat? Probably not – so get the cheaper option.

- **Variety:** A wholesale butcher or fishmonger at a market, or a local butcher's store, will have a wider range of cuts and often offer lower prices. A supermarket, because of space constraints, might not always devote shelf space to a wider (and potentially cheaper) range of cuts. Even if they do have cheaper cuts, some supermarkets know that people will buy meat in a packet from the chiller cabinets rather than look for other cuts from the butcher's counter. So the most choice cuts – and thus the most expensive cuts – are put in the chiller cabinets.

- **In-house Butchers:** Even if you do go to the butcher's counter at a supermarket, remember that, while you are getting fresh, quality-assured meat and a slightly wider range of cuts (for example, you will get liver and kidneys here), he is still there to raise money for the superstore and may not always offer you the cheapest cut each time. (We will look in-depth at preparing cheap cuts of meat in The Cheap Meal Challenge, page 119.)

Specialist Stores

Most supermarkets offer food from around the world to cater for increasingly diverse tastes. But there are also many independent shops and delicatessens that can offer more choice for your money. Just because they look specialist does not mean that they will charge you specialist prices.

Pros and Cons of Specialists

- **Wider range of goods:** African, Asian, Caribbean, Eastern European, Mediterranean, Middle-Eastern and South American shops have their own wholesales, in-depth knowledge of the produce and often a far better range of foodstuffs to suit your differing budgets.

- **'Bulk barn' options:** Chinese, Mexican or Thai food 'bulk barn' stores are excellent for finding the best prices on large quantities of certain products such as sauces or rice, that you would not get at supermarkets. These will last a long time too.

- **Wholesale prices:** Often these stores, because they can buy in bulk at low cost to themselves, can pass on wholesale or near-cost prices to customers, which superstores cannot do.

- **Less purchasing power:** Supermarkets, however, often have the advantage of size and can buy even speciality foods at a better discount, which will be passed on to consumers.

General Stores

Sometimes it is worth buying on impulse when it comes to looking for savings for the family. General stores may not primarily be food stores as they stock all sorts of products, but they

may be the source of some surprise deals.
If you see a deal in an unexpected place, and
you know your family usually buys such items,
then it is worth picking up the deal and crossing
it off the shopping list.

What Sort of Shops Might Have These Surprise Deals?

Poundland, The Pound Shop, the Dollar Store,
Dollarama, Euroland, the 99c Or Less Store to name just a few ... as well as general stores
(make sure you keep your coupons!) and even homeware stores. In such stores, you can
find the following:

- ☑ **confectionery – bulk-buy bags suitable for parties**
- ☑ **packet foods – such as cookies, long-life cakes**
- ☑ **savoury snacks – tins of roast peanuts or crackers**
- ☑ **herbs and spices – usually large bags**

Three Warnings

- ☑ **£1 can be expensive:** Do not be fooled by a bright sticker stating that
  everything in the store is £1 or $1. Sometimes, the foodstuff is cheaper in
  supermarkets. Not everything is a best buy just because it is in a cheap store.

- ☑ **Low quality:** Some of the no-brand, cheap chocolates, wine and champagne are
  not worth buying. This is when a best buy becomes a waste of money because you
  cannot eat the stuff.

- ☑ **Out-of-date:** Always check the sell-by dates on the packets; sometimes they have
  gone past or are fast-approaching the end of their shelf life.

Shopping for Success

During the Second World War, Western countries adopted the slogan 'Digging for victory' to encourage people to help the war effort and feed their families with the fruit of their own labour. Gardens and bomb sites in the UK were turned into allotments and vegetable patches, while farming in the US was required to be more labour-intensive to produce food not just for the US but also for Britain. We are not advocating tearing up your garden, but we are advocating shopping for success. That is, simply, doing all you can to shop wisely, find the best bargains and help meet your budget.

Who is Winning the Price War?

The answer should be – You! But too often, it is the supermarket that wins, not the consumer. Supermarkets, just like any other retailer, want your footfall in these recessionary times, so they will do whatever they can to lure you in. This includes dominant advertising, visible reduction in prices on certain lines and open battles in the media glare. But how can you make the most of this without getting blind-sided by their advertising?

How to Make the Best Out of a Price War

- **Stock up:** Is the foodstuff at the centre of the battle freezable? If so, it is worth buying extra while stocks last.

- **Go further for something you need:** Is it something that you need regularly? If so, it is worth going a little further to save those extra pennies.

✅ **Double up:** Can you redeem club card points against them? There is a double bargain if you can bag a special offer at the same time as gaining loyalty points.

✅ **Shop around:** Who has the largest number of best-price deals? It may not be your usual shop – so be prepared to hunt in a new field.

✅ **Be circumspect:** Remember that not all the prices in the stores are being cut; some are being raised. And sales can sometimes result in you buying food you do not want, need or use.

Reduced to Clear

Most leading supermarkets will have a range of heavily discounted foodstuffs which are approaching their end-of-shelf life. It is also worth asking if you might have a discount on damaged goods.

Get Your Dates Right!

'Sell-by' and 'best-before' dates are not the same as 'use-by' dates:

✅ **Use-by:** A use-by date really means it is the end of a product's life, for example milk or meat.

✅ **Best-before:** This is a guideline; sometimes foodstuff is good for a week after the best-before date.

✅ **Sell-by:** This is an arbitrary measure telling staff when to replenish stock on the shelves, but the food may be good for a week or so yet.

Where to Find

Here are just a few examples of where you can find best-buy prices on reduced-to-clear goods:

- **In-store bakery:** Late at night, supermarkets will often bag up items at knock-down prices.

- **Meat and fish:** If you intend to eat immediately, or freeze, the fresh meat or fish, then it is worth looking for meat at discount prices!

- **Shop-damaged goods:** Dented tins, or individually wrapped chocolate biscuits and other such items may have been dropped, ripped or opened accidentally in-store, but the contents may be undamaged and well within the sell-by date.

- **Last-one-in-the-shop:** Some supermarkets will give you a discount on fruit or veg, especially if some of it looks a little sad.

- **Multi-buys:** If there is a buy-two-get-one-free offer, but some of those items have been discounted, it is worth picking these up as, in some supermarkets, the reduction will apply regardless of the special multi-buy offer.

Special Offers

There are all sorts of special deals around: 'buy-one-get-one-free' ('BOGOF' or 'BOGO') or 'two-for-one' ('2-4-1'), '25 per cent off (or extra)', 'three-for-the-price-of-two' and special half-price lures are becoming a mainstay in supermarkets throughout the year. This sort of deal is great if you really need what is being offered. It is worth planning this strategically, but do not get carried away. Here are some pointers on how to treat special offers:

Catch It While You Can!

If your supermarket is offering one of these deals, grab as much as you can, as this will reduce your shopping bill significantly. For example, if toothpaste is on special offer at just £1 or $1, when it is usually twice that, pick up several tubes. You might have a slightly bigger bill on the day, but over the course of the year you will make huge savings.

Look for Deals on the Family Staples

If you have the freezer space, and you see deals on milk, bread, sausages, bacon and so on, then buy them and save them for another time. This is particularly good for meat and higher-ticket items.

Be Alert

However, there are some things to watch out for, as not every deal may be the best bargain-buy for your family. There have been investigations by various consumer watchdogs about deals such as 2-4-1. They discovered that, while the special offer price takes into account the fact that two items are being sold for the price of one, the price of 'one' is somewhat nominal and has been found to have been raised when used as part of a buy-one-get-one-free deal. While the cost per item is proportionately cheaper than if bought on its own, it is not actually half price, critics claim. So be canny about your purchases.

Extra Free?

25 per cent (or 50 per cent) 'extra' free has also generated flurries of customer letters claiming that stores and manufacturers sometimes put up the price of a product before coming out with a short-term 25-per-cent-extra-free offer. Other consumer champions have seen that the packaging may look a lot larger to entice consumers but, weight-for-weight, another cereal may be offering a better price.

Watch Your Budget

Finally, just because it is a special deal, if it is not on your usual shopping list, do not buy it. It will only break the family food budget – show willpower!

Brand Awareness

Many people like to stick to their well-known brands of pizza or pasta, whether out of habit or because of certain allergies or intolerances. However, leaving aside those who need to use certain brands because of health issues, breaking the habit of always buying the most expensive brand-name goods can save you a lot of money on your household shopping budget.

Variety is the Spice of Life

There is an increasingly wide range of own-brand and no-brand, or 'basics', goods: you can get everything from pasta and margarine to feminine care and toothpaste. Look around for where the deals are to be found. You will be surprised at how much you can get for a lot less when you start to switch from the big-name brands to your store's own brand.

Down-branding Within Superstores

Most supermarkets now have their own premier brand and their basics or no-frills range. Sometimes, down-branding from the household names or the store's own 'premium' brands towards the very plain packaging of the no-frills range can knock between 15 and 30 per cent off a family's annual shopping bill, according to various consumer price websites.

Busting the Brand Myth

Here are a few more pointers to encourage you to save money on your family's average food spend:

 Read the ingredients: The reason why most products from your local store taste similar to leading brands should become obvious from reading the list of ingredients. They are nearly always the same, in more or less the same quantities.

 Taste testing: When eggs, flour, raisins or butter from a store's own-brand range of food is mixed together into a cake, it is very hard for anyone to tell the difference between the own-brand ingredients and the leading brand names.

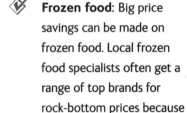

 Frozen food: Big price savings can be made on frozen food. Local frozen food specialists often get a range of top brands for rock-bottom prices because they buy in bulk. But even then, their own brands may work out cheaper.

 Fruit and vegetables: Sometimes there are ranges of packaged fruit and vegetables: a premium brand, the store's own brand and its basic or value brand fruit or vegetables. There is little difference in the taste, particularly when cooked in a casserole.

 Own-brand v. own-brand: There is often little difference between the quality of various supermarkets' own brand goods either. But if a particular store has more own-brand goods that are frequent purchases for your family, then perhaps consider gravitating to that store.

Beware of the 'Budget Blinkers'

You might get so caught up in buying the basics or value, no-frills range that you may miss out on a good bargain elsewhere. Two things to consider:

 Looking out for the best price: For example, a store in Canada was giving out '25c-off' vouchers on its no-frills brand of chicken breasts as shoppers came into the store. Each pack was retailing for CAN$4.50 for a pack of three. But along the next aisle, there was a super sale on the store's upmarket brand of chicken breasts, which were half price and retailing at CAN$3.75 for a pack of three. This was a much better deal.

Ethical considerations: The no-frills range of animal-related produce, meat or eggs may be the cheapest in the shop, but may have been processed using farming techniques with which you might not agree. No-brand eggs, for example, are usually from battery or caged hens. It might be worth paying more for conscience's sake.

Making the Most of Deals and Offers

In addition to the 2-4-1s, do not forget to get as much as you can out of coupons, points and other deals, as well as your loyalty cards:

Junk Mail

Do not throw away any marketing that comes through your door before you have checked it. There may be some discount coupons that may be useful. Keep them in your purse for when you go shopping.

Look Online

Sometimes money-off vouchers are on independent websites or the store's own website. You can print these off and use them against certain items. Beware, though; not all the vouchers may be for everyone to use. The same applies to discount delivery codes, which are internet codes that can cut the price of home shopping.

Take a Raincheck

Ask for what are commonly called 'raincheck' vouchers – if a special offer item is not in stock, the store manager might give you a voucher entitling you to the same deal at a later date.

Points Promotions

In-store deals offering extra points for a particular product are a great way to save for that rainy day or big celebration.

Free Samples

Do not throw these away. They are great to use for a rainy day when you run out of teabags, or to cut down one month on more expensive household items such as washing powder.

Surveys

If you are offered the chance to win free shopping for a year just by filling in a survey, then go for it. What have you got to lose? Or, what could you gain?

Making the Most of Your Loyalty Cards

You are earning points, so make the most of them by spending them to defray the cost of your shopping every now and then. If you can collect Air Miles on these cards, even better – your food shopping is helping to pay for your holiday to Florida.

Transport Costs

Thankfully, by the end of 2008, fuel prices had halved from their 2007 highs. This has been no small relief for families whose cars were beginning to be a bigger drain on their weekly finances than their student teenagers. There are still some ways to help reduce expenditure on the cost of

motoring, parking and fuel, however, which will help offset the cost of travelling to do the family food shop:

 shop with a friend and share the car costs

 look for special deals on using your loyalty card at the store fuel station

 collect Air Miles at the store's own pumps as well as in store

 shop from home once in a while

No Such Thing as a Free Lunch

Remember this mantra! The shops are all telling us they can help us beat inflation. But a supermarket's aim is not to help customers out of a tight spot, but to make us spend money in their stores. As a final checklist to help you decide where to shop, consider the following:

 Distance: If you have to drive further to get to the best price, are you spending more on petrol than you are saving?

 Loyalty: It may be worth taking advantage of being loyal to your store, rather than chasing short-term price cuts elsewhere. If you use a club or points card regularly, how much have you saved on it? Is it worth switching stores now, or maximizing your points?

 Check everything: Each store claims to be cheaper – but how true is this? Prices change quicker than TV advertising – have a look yourself before you do your weekly shop.

 Look further: Do not just compare what the stores are advertising, compare the price of everything you buy regularly. Item for item, which works out cheaper? Which store will give you the best prices across a range of goods?

A Few Last Things to Remember

It is more than possible to shop for success without stressing or spending hours scrutinizing every piece of advertising material or points promotion that comes through your door.

And once you have got into the habit of knowing where to check for the latest prices, and when are the best times to shop to make the most of any deals and discounts, it will become second nature to you.

Only Once or Twice a Year is Fine

It is worth taking time to learn where the best bargains are to be found for your family's food items. But you will not have to do this each time you shop: just doing it once or twice a year can help you work out whether you are getting more bang(ers) for your buck.

Be Prepared to Change Your Habits

Switching your shop, planning ahead and setting a budget are not easy things to do, but once you get into a routine, saving money will become second nature. Expect to put some serious thinking in for the first month of your new family shopping and cooking regime. After that, you will really notice the benefits of a healthier and slightly wealthier family food budget.

Ask, and You May Receive

It is always worth asking around to find out what tips other families could share with you. Other people you know may have found bargains at stores you have never really explored. For example, one young woman from the Netherlands, Anna, comes from a large family of eight and has learned to cook and bake on a tight budget. She always produces the finest meals for her student friends, although she works for a charity on a very low salary. When

asked how she could afford to entertain, she simply replied, 'I know what I want to cook, and how many people I am cooking for. So I get the right amount of ingredients from Lidl.' Based on her till receipts, she can cook a two-course meal for four people for about £6 (US$8.50). Why not ask your friends not only where they shop, but for their money-saving recipes?

Thinking Outside of the Trolley

For those of you concerned not only by the food budget but by the number of pesticides in food or the soaring cost of energy, there are many ways to cut back on expenditure on the raw ingredients. One of the most popular ways to be 'organic' and to reduce costs is to grow your own vegetables. If you are blessed with a garden, a shared allotment or even a window box, you can become a mini-farmer and bring your own produce to the table.

The Kitchen Garden

Many vegetables are easy and cheap to grow, requiring little attention except a good watering now and then and some decent soil. You do not need to have a perfect climate as many of these plants are hardy and can endure long winters, as long as you wrap them up against the snow and frost. So, if you can manage to grow your own, that is a lot of fruit and vegetables that you will no longer have to buy! And those who do grow their own say that the quality of the taste is so much better than ones found in supermarkets or convenience stores.

What Can You Grow?

There are so many things that you can grow in your back garden, greenhouse or allotment:

 Vegetables: Aubergines/eggplants, broccoli, brussels sprouts, cabbages, carrots, cauliflowers, cucumbers, courgettes/zucchini, onions, marrows, parsnips, potatoes, pumpkins, most beans, tomatoes, turnips, radishes, squashes, swedes....

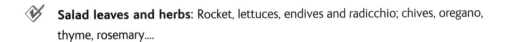

- **Salad leaves and herbs:** Rocket, lettuces, endives and radicchio; chives, oregano, thyme, rosemary....

- **Fruit:** Blackberries (if you do not mind the plants being plain old pernicious 'weeds' for the rest of the year), blueberries (these can be grown wild), raspberries (these will require more care), strawberries, watermelons....

Plant a Tree!

The northern hemisphere is great for family favourites. You may have a high initial expenditure on the cost of buying a small tree, but the actual upkeep is not as time-consuming as caring for garden vegetables. With good planting and a decent amount of rainfall, within a few years you can enjoy:

- apples
- apricots
- pears
- cherries
- figs
- plums
- peaches

The Herb Box

Herbs can be costly, especially fresh ones such as basil, parsley, rosemary or mint. But these can all be grown very cheaply, not only in your garden, but in a window box or even in containers on a windowsill, benefiting from the warmth and humidity of your kitchen. With careful nurturing, these can last a long time. Bear in mind that herbs need:

Light: The herbs will need a sufficient amount of direct sunlight; if you are growing them in a shed, then use fluorescent lights. Not all herbs need as much sun as you might think, however: sage, rosemary, thyme, french tarragon and oregano like full sun, but parsley, chervil, rocket, sorrel, mustard and mizuna like partial shade.

Moisture: Herbs must be sufficiently watered when the top layer of soil is dry; and they must not be in an environment that is too hot and dry (if your kitchen or planting environment is too dry, keep a little pot of water near the plants).

Decent soil: Use a soil-based compost rather than peat-based.

Regular checks: Keep an eye out for aphids or other mites and discard dead leaves.

Easy Herbs to Grow

Many, like mint, require little attention – except for some serious pruning before they take over the whole window box.

Perennials: Herbs such as lavender and rosemary can be potted from fresh – either bought or from someone's garden. These can be kept indoors.

Annuals: Herbs such as basil, mint, chervil, parsley, dill and oregano can be started from seeds in small containers indoors.

The Shared Allotment or Community Garden

Families in apartments without gardens may find that buying or renting an allotment and sharing it with friends and neighbours (or joining a community garden project) is the only way to really get into growing their own vegetables. Sharing helps to spread the cost and results in less time and input per person, while you still get to enjoy the work of your own hand and learn to grow and care for seasonal vegetables without having to buy them. It also provides some great outdoor exercise for the family! However, there are some points to ponder:

Difficult to get one:
There is a long waiting list
for allotments, of several
years, so put your name
down early.

 Use it! If you have an
allotment, make sure you
are dedicated to using it,
or it is a waste of money
and good ground.

 Relationships: If you
share an allotment, make
sure you have a good
relationship with the
people with whom you are
sharing, and that everyone
understands when and
how it is to be used.

More Information

For more information on growing your own or maintaining an allotment,
check out the following websites:

 www.freshliving.com
www.growyourown.co.uk
www.gardenhealth.com
www.growingherbs.org.uk

 www.thegardeners-directory.co.uk
www.gardenersnet.com/veggies
www.communitygarden.org

Family
Needs

PACKED WITH
• MONEY •
SAVING
IDEAS & TIPS

Health and Wealth

Sadly, research and received wisdom shows that many believe that the ability to eat healthily is a privilege reserved for the wealthy in society. But it is perfectly possible for people who are having to live on an ever-tightening income to be able to cook healthy, delicious, filling meals for their families without breaking their budgets. We want to help families avoid the 'convenience food trap' that cash-strapped people fall into in the mistaken belief that these foods are cheaper.

The Statistics

On both sides of the Atlantic, academic studies show that women and children living on lower incomes are likely to have higher instances of obesity. Let us look at some statistics.

Obesity and Low-income Families

Childhood obesity is at its highest ever levels in many Western countries. According to the World Health Organization, 'In 2007, an estimated 22 million children under the age of 5 years were overweight throughout the world. More than 75 per cent of overweight and obese children live in low- and middle-income countries. Overweight and obese children are likely to stay obese into adulthood and more likely to develop non-communicable diseases like diabetes and cardiovascular diseases at a younger age. Overweight [sic] and obesity, as well as their related diseases, are largely preventable. Prevention of childhood obesity therefore needs high priority.'

This information, published in 2008, showed to the world's leaders a clear link between poverty and obesity. This was explored by Western countries to see if there were a link between the lower-income families and rising obesity and weight-related health problems. Health services and academics on both sides of the pond found that there were food-related health problems, rising malnutrition and weight gain among women and children who were living on very tight budgets.

Expert View

The Zaccheus Trust 2000 is a charity that seeks to eradicate social imbalance and to restore health and social care to the most deprived. In a letter to UK newspaper *The Times*, The Rev Paul Nicolson, chairman of the charity, says, 'The incomes of the poorest mothers and their children are more often than not reduced by debts imposed by the State, such as tax credit overpayments, rent and council tax arrears, or because of borrowing at high interest rates for expenditure on clothes, utilities and transport. The weekly repayments reduce the already inadequate share of income available to buy a healthy diet, so cheap, filling and fattening meals are the affordable option. The plight of those mothers and children [...] is a scandal of international proportions.' (October 23, 2007)

Breaking the Link Between Budget and Bad Food

These facts are startling and it seems that families on the lowest incomes and those who are forced by circumstance to live on an ever-tightening budget are torn between the need to buy a filling meal and to buy only fresh, healthy produce.

The Evil of Advertising

This perception is not helped by advertising. It seems that every time we go to a supermarket or watch TV commercials expounding the price cuts across convenience food, we are led down a path signposted towards 'cheap, filling and fattening meals'. For instance, items such as pizzas, oven chips, ready-made burgers and frozen roast potatoes are retailed at £1/$1 – a bargain for a time-poor, cash-conscious family.

Examples of Convenience Food

This is only a brief list, not exhaustive by any means; and it is worrying how many of these find their way into our shopping trolleys:

- ready meals (for oven or microwave)
- pizzas
- oven chips/fries
- frozen 'ready-made' roast potatoes
- tinned soup, meat, vegetables
- instant mashed potato
- pre-cooked burgers, meat patties
- crispy pancakes
- fish fingers
- frozen cakes
- breaded turkey or chicken – drummers, kievs, etc.
- burgers
- sugary, 'easy' breakfast items
- packaged cakes, cookies, bakery items

Caught in a Trap?

This is not to suggest that everyone who is on a strict budget is reduced by state and circumstance to eat the cheapest and most unhealthy meals, or that obesity only strikes those who cannot afford to eat fresh fruit and vegetables every day. But it is easy for time-pressed families living on a budget to fall into the trap posed by supermarkets' 'conditioning' that says convenience food is a good thing for the wallet and the tastebuds. It is not.

A Lesson to Be Learned

Hopefully, the following chapters will show that it is possible to put together a budget, stick to it, shop well and eat healthily. Another lesson from history: in 1949, while rationing was still on and countries around the world were struggling with huge debts in the aftermath of the Second World War, the proportion of children with obesity was negligible. In 1970, according to the US Center for Nutrition Policy and Promotion, this figure was 7 per cent. Some 30 years on, this figure has risen to 20–30 per cent in the US and 25 per cent in the UK (according to WorldPress.com and the NHS). So how can we, in our indebted, credit-crunch world, learn to avoid so-called cheap but cholesterol-laden convenience food?

Convenience is a Myth

Grabbing a pizza out of the freezer every now and then is a convenience for families pressed for time and money. Such items are usually inexpensive, can be bought in bulk and frozen, meaning when the parents have no time prepare food, out come the 'convenience' items. Sadly, 'convenience' has too ready an appeal in this world of instant cash, instant credit, instant coffee and instant communication. We want it now and we want it yesterday, and it cannot cost us any more than we need to spend.

Detox Your Head

Why do stores charge so little for convenience food? Because they know advertising works. These foods taste nice, are produced for a fraction of the seemingly low cost the stores charge and can hook in the customer who thinks they are getting a bargain. No student would turn up his nose at an offer for ready-made noodles. But once in the store, there are so many temptations, and not everything is really as cheap as it looks. In fact, stocking up on 'cheap' freezer fillers works out more expensive:

- **No leftover food or ingredients**: There are rarely any leftovers, certainly not from ready meals. What is more, there are no 'raw' ingredients remaining for you to use in another meal, so you have to keep buying more of the convenience food.

- **Extras**: You usually feel the need to accompany a ready meal with something else – such as 'lasagne and chips' or 'pizza and garlic bread' (both are a carbohydrate overload!). Why not swap the chips and garlic bread for some fresh salad? Kids may hate the bitter tang of some lettuce, but they like cherry tomatoes and grated carrot....

- **Empty padding**: You may feel full, but not satisfied, as your body is lacking in certain nutrients.

- **Do not be fooled**: You might be misled by bright yellow stickers in the store proclaiming that everything is £1 or $1, but you will be able to get many items for less than this (and fresher) elsewhere. For example, broccoli may be priced at £1/$1 in a store that is advertising pizzas or chips for the same price. But you can buy broccoli for half this price in other stores or in a local market.

- **They will get you somehow**: Nobody is going to offer you something for nothing. There is no such thing as a free lunch, even for journalists. Once the shop has got you in with half-price pizzas, it will charge you higher prices on other goods.

Healthier Can Be Cheaper

It is better to buy versatile food that can last for several meals, rather than stock up on one-meal-at-a-time foodstuffs. While there is a place for a pizza or ready-made burgers within a family's food plan, these do not really save money in the long term as, once they are gone, they are gone and you will need to keep re-stocking. Buying the essentials such as rice or pasta and adding fresh vegetables that will last for two or three meals means you get variety, healthy options and longer-term savings.

Don't Go Cold Turkey on the Twizzlers!

Fox News ran a whole series of reports in June 2008 on new, improved junior-high and high-school menus to prove that, although nutritional meals were more expensive, there were ways of cutting the cost of a good meal. UK chef Jamie Oliver also had aspirations for healthier school meals. What he did was to completely remove all breaded food (which was often fried) and replace it with healthy options. It was nicknamed a 'war on the turkey twizzler', the eponymous foodstuff being a twisted mass of re-formed turkey, coated in breadcrumbs.

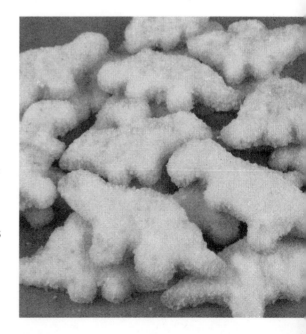

The Reaction?

The reaction to Oliver's regime was that many children hated the new-taste canteen. It was a sudden change and seemed to be a 'punishment'. There was video footage of parents pushing hot burgers and French fries through the school railings to their (often overweight) disgruntled teenagers. The idea was right – get these youngsters to eat well – but the methods were wrong and had the opposite effect.

The Point Is ...

Do not completely cut out these convenience foods, at least not immediately. If used in the right way, they are cheap and easy – and once children have had a taste of them they will demand more! The point is to create balanced family meals that enable them to get their 'five a day' of fruit and veg without spending hours slaving over a hot stove or shelling out on the finest organic vegetables.

Using Convenience Food Wisely

Balance is key. You will not save money in the long term if you rely on convenience food, and you will not have a healthy family. But if you use it within your weekly meal plan in a sensible way, you will find it a valuable means of reducing your family's food bill without increasing their waistlines.

Convenience Food as Part of a Healthy Meal Plan

Imagine a week of the main family meals. You can introduce convenience food for two or three days, as long as it has been balanced with healthy options. Here is a rough idea of how to do this:

 Pizza: Instead of giving each family member a whole small pizza, buy one large one and serve each person a couple of slices, together with a lot of fresh salad (if you make this yourself, you will know what they do or do not like in it). You can also accompany this with a little French bread topped with chopped tomatoes, mozzarella and onions – so much healthier than packaged garlic bread! Any leftover pizza becomes a great lunch item the next day.

Breaded meat or vegetarian dishes: Instead of serving these with chips, serve them with fresh mashed potatoes or new potatoes sprinkled with mint, accompanied by peas, sweetcorn and carrots.

Chips/fries: Try cooking fresh fish without batter, or using the chips alongside a lovely home-made casserole that has lots of vegetables in it.

Cans: Add lentils or fresh vegetables to tinned soup to give it more substance and flavour; use tinned meats alongside a fresh salad and home-made coleslaw for a light yet filling lunch; incorporate tinned vegetables into sauces and gravies for cheap and easy stews, pie fillings and casseroles.

The Dieticians' Challenge

The following tips, used as part of the WeightWatchers® and other good nutritionists' approaches to combating obesity, are brilliant ways of gauging food intake. They can help to ensure that your family is not overloading on carbohydrates, fats and sugars at the expense of vitamins, nutrients and healthy food. These can be used also to lose a little extra weight without forcing you or your family on to a dangerous crash diet.

Think of Your Plate as a Clock

When out in a restaurant or when served a large plateful of food such as pasta or paella, mentally divide the plate into quarter-hours. Starting at 12, eat a quarter of the meal until 3 o'clock, then another quarter until 6 o'clock and so on until you feel full. Do not keep eating once you feel full and satisfied.

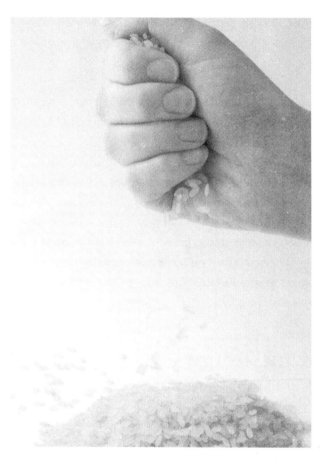

Rule-by-fist

A portion for adults is equivalent to the size of your fist. This will cut down on a lot of unnecessary food waste, for example, a fist-sized portion of rice will be satisfying. A fistful serving of pasta, together with salad, will suffice your body's dietary needs.

Serve in Thirds

To balance the amount of carbohydrate intake, you might like to think in thirds. For example, serve one-third of mashed potato, one-third of vegetables and one-third of meat. You should never have just carbs for your main meal, just as it can be dangerous to eat nothing but salad.

Ways to Save

The three rules above are great for:

 reducing food wastage
 helping to plan meals that are healthy
 preventing you from using too much food at once
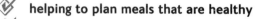 and therefore, saving you money

Case Study: The Pearsons

Colin and Rosemary Pearson and their twin boys, Robert and Beck, often use convenience food but they make sure it is part of a varied and balanced diet, as they try to balance their food spend against making sure they can eat healthily. Colin says, 'We don't set a budget but we do monitor it closely. We probably spend about $500 (£360) a month on food, but we only tend to get what we need. We estimate that, per person, we spend between $3 (£2) and $6 (£4) on weekdays and Sundays respectively. We shop at a superstore that does significant discounts and we do buy frozen desserts and convenience food. Not all the food we eat is healthy, as preparing a meal from scratch, healthy or otherwise, is always more time-consuming than opening a packet pizza. So we will use things such as pizza when pressed for time, but we always try to balance this with plenty of salad or fruit for dessert and, when we have time, we will cook a healthy meal.'

Catering for Allergies and Intolerances

Families are increasingly having to deal with children and young people who are born with allergies or who develop intolerances to certain food groups. These can range from an inability to process certain ingredients to violent reactions or severe digestive problems. While these can be treated medically, or sometimes diminish over time, they can also result in restricted diets or the need for special food items – and because these food items are less likely to be as much in demand, shops and outlets stocking these will price them higher.

Allergy v. Intolerance

These are both types of sensitivity to food and can have a long-term effect on people. But the former can be life-threatening, while the latter tends to affect health to a lesser extent.

The Food Allergy

When someone has a food allergy, their immune system reacts to a particular food and treats it as an 'unsafe' or 'unwelcome' intruder into the body. So if someone has a severe food allergy, this can cause them to go into anaphylactic shock – a life-threatening reaction. This means that people with food allergies, such as peanut or shellfish allergy, need to be extremely careful about what they eat.

The Food Intolerance

Food intolerance does not involve the immune system and is generally not life-threatening. But if someone eats a food they are intolerant to, this could make them feel ill or affect their long-term health. These can cause or exacerbate problems such as irritable bowel syndrome (IBS), for example, or create ulcers.

Which Foods Cause Allergic or Intolerant Reactions?

Any food group could potentially cause an allergic or intolerant reaction in someone, depending on their genetic make-up. Many allergies in children will dissipate over time as the body changes and develops, except for the most serious ones, unfortunately. In adults, most allergic reactions are to peanuts, nuts, fish, shellfish and wheat. The most common foods that cause 90 per cent of allergic reactions are:

- cereals containing gluten (including wheat, rye, barley and oats)
- lupin (used in some flours)
- fish
- crustaceans (including crabs and prawns)
- celery
- eggs
- milk
- peanuts (groundnuts or monkey nuts)
- hazelnuts, almonds and walnuts
- sesame seeds
- soya
- sulphur dioxide or sulphites

Know Your Enemy

It is not easy to avoid the 'hidden' allergy-inducing foodstuffs. But knowing in advance what to look for can help you plan your shopping and meal preparation. This can also help you work out which stores offer the best prices and the widest selection on the safest food for your family. Here, we look in more detail about various allergies and intolerances.

Cereal Allergy

Different types of cereal (wheat, rye, barley, oats, maize/corn and rice can cause reactions in some people. It can be difficult to avoid maize or corn as these ingredients are included in many food products:

 biscuits/cookies
 batters
 cake mixes
 wafers

Coeliac Disease and Gluten Allergy

Coeliac disease is a sensitivity to gluten, a protein found in wheat and other cereals. It is not an allergy which will cause anaphylaxis. However, people who have this disease (and usually do not know it) and eat food containing gluten will suffer damage to the lining of the intestine, which stops the body from absorbing nutrients. This can lead to diarrhoea, weight loss and, eventually, malnutrition. Foods to avoid are:

 rye
 wheat
 barley
 bread
 pasta
pizza

pastry

 biscuits

 cakes

 food in breadcrumbs

 alcoholic drinks made from barley (beer, lager, barley water)

Wheat Allergy

This is not the same as Coeliac disease. Wheat allergy is usually caused by a protein within gluten, called gliadin. Although the same restrictions often apply on what food people with Coeliac disease and those with wheat allergy may eat, not all gluten-free foods are suitable for wheat allergy sufferers. Always check the label.

Lupin Allergy

Lupins are used widely in Europe and the US and Canada for flour, but not so commonly in the UK. The lupin is a flower similar to a foxglove, and is related to the legume family, which includes beans, lentils and peanuts. Seeds from some strains of lupin are ground to make flour, which, in some people with sensitivities to it, can cause reactions including anaphylaxis.

Fish and Shellfish Allergy

Shellfish is a major cause of food allergy for adults, as well as 'white' fish such as cod or haddock. Cooking does not destroy all the allergens in fish. Also there is the threat of fish poisoning, which is caused by fish and shellfish having increased levels of histamine if they are not processed properly. This can produce reactions similar to allergic reactions, but can affect anyone, not just those with a known fish or shellfish allergy. Shellfish are crustaceans and molluscs (of which a snail is one member of the family) and include:

 clams

 cockles

 crabs

 crayfish

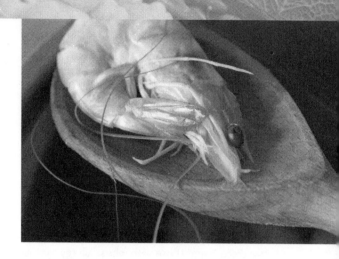

 langoustines
 lobsters
 mussels
 oysters
 prawns
 shrimp
 scallops
 winkles

Celery Allergy

Celery (the stem of the vegetable) is common in salads. The root of the celery, celeriac, is a popular flavouring and ingredient in soups and meals. Both the celery (stem) and celeriac (root) can cause oral allergy syndrome, which ranges from a burning in the lips, mouth and pharynx, through to anaphylaxis at the most extreme. As people switch from standard salt to 'healthier' seasonings, beware of celery salt being added as flavourings or preservatives to items such as stock cubes or stuffing. Celeriac as a spice is often added to soups and packaged food.

Fruit and Vegetable Allergy

This is mild and results usually in a rash, or blisters where the food touches the lips and mouth, or sometimes the skin on the hands. It might also affect those who are allergic to pollen, and those who suffer from hayfever symptoms. Known fruit and vegetable allergies include: apples, celery, kiwi fruit, peaches, peppers, strawberries and tomatoes. The risk can be lowered by:

 Cooking: Generally, cooking fruit and vegetables makes them less likely to cause an allergic reaction.

 Heat treatments: Pasteurization and other heat treatments (which are used, for example, on fruit juices) have the same effect on some vegetables.

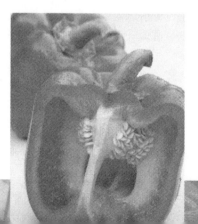

- ☑ **Check for ripeness**: How ripe a fruit or vegetable is can also make a difference; the riper the bell pepper, the more likely the reaction, for example.

Latex-food Syndrome

This lesser-known syndrome affects some people who are allergic to Latex clothing. Latex contains many allergens, similar to those found in some foods such as apples, avocados, bananas, carrots, celery, cherries, chestnuts, coconuts, kiwis, mangos, paprika and strawberries. This is called latex-food syndrome. In the same way, people who are allergic to these foods may also react to latex.

Additives Intolerance

Often there are many preservatives, flavourings and colourings and other additives in packaged or ready-made food products. Altogether there are more than 1500 different types of additive. Not all additives are unnatural, although some are. In the UK, these are often simply bundled together under the generic terms of E-numbers, but there are many different types. In other parts of the world, the letter is left off the number, so Tartrazine, for example, may appear as E102 or simply as 102. People who react to additives may normally have asthma or other allergies already. Reactions to additives usually bring on an asthma attack or cause nettle rash. Examples of additives in food include:

- ☑ **Sulphites**: These are found in food such as burgers and soft drinks, and are naturally occurring in wine (though they add them to wine too).

- ☑ **Benzoates**: These are found naturally in honey and fruit, and are usually used as preservatives.

- ☑ **Tartrazine (E102)**: This is a yellow colour added to drinks and sauces, although it is not so commonly added to food nowadays. It is an example of one of the more potentially harmful E-numbers.

Egg Allergy

The main causes of this are three proteins in the white of eggs, ovomucoid, ovalbumin and conalbumin. Cooking can destroy some of these allergens, but not all, which means that some people might react to raw eggs (found in icing/confectioners' sugar and mayonnaise, for example) but not cooked eggs. Children often grow out of an egg allergy by the time they are three or four.

Milk Allergy and Intolerance

Milk allergy, often called 'dairy allergy', can be quite serious and debilitating when it comes to cooking and preparing the family meal. Many people are born allergic to the protein in cow's milk, which can bring on symptoms such as rashes, diarrhoea, vomiting, stomach cramps and difficulty in breathing. Rarely, it could cause anaphylaxis. Some people are allergic to any dairy, including goat's milk and cheese, and also to buffalo mozzarella. When you think of all the family meals that involve these ingredients (pizza, some pasta dishes, creamy soups), it shows just how much forward planning you need to do to ensure that your family is kept safe. Those who are allergic to cow's milk are likely to be allergic to:

 cheese made from cow's milk
 yoghurt
 cream
 cakes or pastries made with cow's milk
 ice cream made with cow's milk
 processed meat products (pâté, some breadcrumbed meat pieces, sliced 'luncheon' meat, some burgers and frankfurters do often use milk products in the ingredients)

Lactose Intolerance

People often confuse milk allergy with lactose intolerance, but this is caused by the sugar (lactose) naturally occurring in milk. Adults whose intake of milk has decreased over a lifetime and who are deficient in the enzyme lactase are those most likely to develop this intolerance, which causes bloating and diarrhoea.

Tree Nut Allergy

Tree nut allergies (that is, reactions to nuts other than *peanuts*, which are in fact legumes) last throughout someone's life and can cause anaphylaxis, sometimes (but rarely) leading to death. This is why it is so important that food is labelled correctly, and that the packet states that a certain food might have come into contact with nuts in the same factory. The most common tree nuts to cause allergic reactions are almonds, Brazil nuts, cashews, hazelnuts (sometimes called corn nuts or hob-nuts), macadamia nuts, pecans, pistachios and walnuts – and sometimes pine nuts. Watch out for:

 oils, spreads and sauces made from nuts
 flavourings derived from nuts
 crushed nuts used to decorate food such as cakes

Peanut Allergy

Known as monkey nuts or groundnuts, this legume (part of the 'bean' family) is a well-known allergy-inducing food. They can cause severe anaphylaxis because they contain several allergens which are not only not removed by roasting or cooking, but can be enhanced by the heating process. Even small amounts, or a trace on a knife used to cut something containing peanuts that contaminates food eaten by someone with this allergy can make them react. Watch out for:

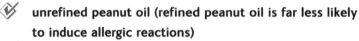

- unrefined peanut oil (refined peanut oil is far less likely to induce allergic reactions)
- sweets containing peanuts or unrefined peanut oil
- chocolates made in the same machinery where peanut confectionery is also processed

Coconut Allergy

Coconut allergy is rare, but it can cause reactions (such as anaphylaxis) in people who may be sensitive. Although coconut is not a nut, some people who are allergic to nuts may also be allergic. Some people who are allergic to latex may react to coconut too. Watch out for:

- coconut milk (often used in curries)
- coconut added to 'tropical' fruit juice
- desiccated coconut sprinkled on cakes and cookies
- coconut added as an ingredient or flavouring to other foods

Rice Allergy

Less common than other staple foods such as wheat and barley, rice allergy can cause reactions in some people. Those living in areas where it is grown and who are allergic to it may also suffer from hayfever when they inhale its pollen.

Sesame Allergy

This is becoming more common in the West as sesame becomes part of everyday cooking and snacking. Allergic reactions to the proteins inside sesame seeds can take the form of anaphylaxis. Those who are allergic to sesame may also react to poppy seeds, hazelnuts and kiwi fruit. Try to avoid:

- mediterranean dishes such as houmous and tahini dips
- snackbread or cakes with sesame seeds
- sesame seed oil and cooking spray (it is unrefined)

Soya

Many toddlers might be allergic to soya, but tend to grow out of it. However, some adults are still allergic to it and it has similar effects to milk allergy. These can take the form of anaphylaxis (rarely), breathing difficulties, diarrhoea, stomach cramps, rashes or vomiting. Soya can be put into more food products than you might realize. These include:

- bakery produce (ask if there is no label)
- cereals
- drinks
- ice cream
- margarine and low-fat spreads
- pasta
- processed meats
- soya flour (used for longevity)
- soya protein (used as a meat substitute and in some processed meat products)
- sweets

Case Study

It is not easy to budget when catering for severe intolerances and allergic reactions, as there is a natural limit on what you can buy and prepare for your child. One family has proved that they can do it, but it requires a lot of thought and attention.

Meet the Wardours

Margaret Wardour, 10, is like any other child: active, fun-loving, mischievous and bright.

But she is also severely restricted in what she can eat, having developed several serious allergies from birth. Her father Michael, mother Caroline and sister Grace, 7, have never had any allergies or intolerances, so it was a shock to the parents when Margaret took ill suddenly a few days after she started to eat solid food.

Dealing with Margaret's Allergies

Caroline explains, 'Some food would give Margaret a violent reaction within about half an hour (dairy and egg). Others will gradually make her skin more flared up (wheat). Then, there is the additional factor that, as her body is not challenged with new foods very often, if she eats something new, or a different make of the same food, then her body can react to it, even if she does not have an intolerance or an allergy to it. We are therefore faced with having to give her tiny amounts of anything new, then watching for a reaction, then gradually increasing the size of the portion and watching again for a reaction, until eventually she might be having a proper portion for a child of her age. It is time-consuming, laborious, requires careful planning and persistence and can be stressful.

How Allergies Affect the Food Budget

'Our food budget is huge. Maggie has nearly everything organic as I am convinced that there are fewer pesticides etc. used on everything when it is organic. Also the wheat-free, dairy-free stuff is all more expensive. The cost is offset as we rarely go out to eat at a restaurant and we rarely go abroad on holiday (and we have never been abroad successfully for more than a week) as carting all Maggie's food is just not worth the hassle and you rarely get the same make of product overseas.

Hope for the Future

'It is hard work living with allergies and there are a whole load of psychological issues that come along with it too. However, it is nothing compared to what many families who have sick children have to endure. Margaret can participate in most aspects of life and her allergies mean that she eats good quality food so she won't suffer from obesity. My hope is that as Margaret grows older she will be willing to try the foods that are unlikely to give her a reaction and that she will want to expand the variety of food she eats.'

Margaret's Meals

☑️ **Breakfast:** Wheat-free cereal (Mesa Sunrise), 2 pieces of organic Duchy ham and a mug of warm Rice Dream (a milk substitute), sometimes with a spoonful of Dove plain chocolate sprinkles.

☑️ **Snack:** Apples (the only fresh fruit Maggie will eat).

☑️ **Lunch and dinner:** Potato, rice or rice/corn pasta, with one or two veg and a protein such as baked meat or fish.

☑️ **Dessert:** One of her limited range of wheat-free biscuits and a piece of plain dark chocolate (also from a limited selection).

Kids Out and About

It is not easy to keep an eye on what kids are eating when they go to friends' houses, to school or away on summer camp. While most carers, teachers and youth leaders are aware of and cater for those with allergies and sensitivities to certain ingredients, you cannot be sure that food is not shared around by the young people themselves.

School

Caroline says, 'Our selection of school for Margaret took into consideration that the school only catered for packed lunches. Margaret originally went to a school that had hot lunches. We had to get a doctor's letter to give her the right to take in a packed lunch and she ended up with quite a few emotional issues relating to feeling the odd one out that were challenging to deal with.'

Ways to Provide Meals (When You Are Not There)

You cannot always be around your child. But there are ways of helping them to help themselves, without resorting to shelling out high amounts of cash so they can buy the food they need at sky-high prices.

- **The packed lunch:** Unless the child is visiting families who know you well, and buy the same brands and type of food as your child eats, then provide snacks and a packed lunch, including the drink and dessert.

- **Make treats for sharing:** Rather than have your child lose out when cakes are shared, why not bake some cookies or a cake that takes your child's allergies into consideration? This can be shared out, provided that your child knows to ask if his or her friends also have intolerances.

- **Learning to ask:** Teach them how to ask and check for themselves about different brands or new food items.

- **Teach to teach others:** Teach them some easy recipes so they can cook or help an adult to cook for them.

Budget-friendly Tips for Allergies and Intolerances

Obviously, catering for someone with serious intolerances and allergies increases your expenditure greatly by limiting what you can buy. However, where you can, try to save money and budget for meals for family members suffering from allergies and intolerances. The following might help:

Check the Labels

When buying sauces, soups, pre-packaged meals or desserts, always check the labels for information. Legally, manufacturers must declare whether the food contains, or may have come into contact with, allergy-inducing food. This way food should not go to waste.

Stick to Your Brand

When you find something that does not evoke allergic reactions, try to look for deals on those particular brands. Many of these brands might be more expensive because of the more rigorous processes in manufacturing the food so, if you see them on special offer, stock up. Try looking on websites to see which stores might have a better price on them.

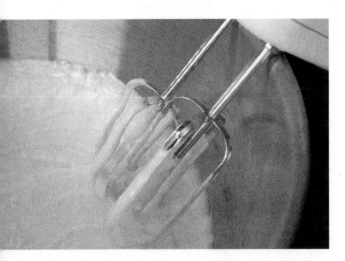

Cook and Grow Your Own

Making your own sauces, growing your own organic vegetables and baking your own cakes will save you money in the long term and give your family peace of mind with the knowledge that there are no bad additives or pesticides in the food. Hints and tips about cooking and growing your own are given in The Family Kitchen, pages 102–173.

Find Shared Ground

Rather than cook two separate meals all the time to cater for someone with an allergy, try to find common ground – meals that the whole family will enjoy together. This will also help not to make one member of the family feel 'different' or 'excluded', while cutting your budget and saving you time in preparation.

Find Time to Test

Use school holidays as a time to test new foods for children, without the pressures of taking the children to school. It also enables you to check more closely for reactions.

Gradual Exposure

Increase the range of food slowly. For example, introduce new fruit through the medium of smoothies or puddings, but do not buy extra – use what the rest of the family already eats.

Boost the Needed Nutrients

For example, boost protein intake through meat, fish or soya for people with eczema, as protein helps to rebuild the damaged skin cells. This is food the whole family can share. Try to develop ways of using cheaper cuts of meat if the sufferer can eat meat (*see* pages 200–219).

Check Whether You Are Overly Limiting the Diet

Caroline adds, 'There is always the awareness that Margaret might not be eating something that she used to be allergic to but may not be allergic to any more. We may be limiting her diet in a way that her body does not need us to limit it.' If so, you might be able to buy cheaper brands of food to help lower the household spend.

Finding out More

For more information on food allergies and intolerances, and how to look out for the 'hidden nasties' in other foods, these websites may be helpful:

 www.foodsmatter.com   **www.eatwell.gov.uk**

Age and Health Requirements

It is not only people with allergies or intolerances who need to be catered for; different dietary constraints may imposed for health reasons. It could be diabetic complaints or something lovely, such as having a baby! Regardless of age, there are still various health demands that can put extra strains on the budget. This section looks at catering for pregnancy, toddlers, teenagers, diabetic diets, heart complaints, old age and stress.

Eating for Two (or Three?)

It is a common myth that pregnant women have to eat twice as much because they are 'eating for two'. Unborn babies will absorb the nutrients and goodness they need from their mothers' food, while newborns will also take what they need from their mothers' milk. But there are needs (and restrictions) on what pregnant and breastfeeding mothers can (or should) eat, and this can have an impact on the budget.

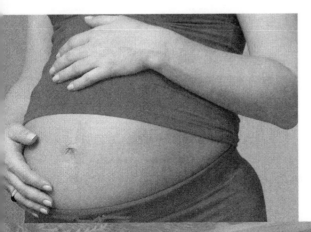

What to Avoid in Pregnancy

If you feel like eating pickle ice cream, that is entirely up to you and there is a lot to be said medically for eating what your body is craving and telling you to eat. However, remember you are also responsible for the little one inside you – and for your own good health. Unfortunately, there are quite a few items you should avoid:

- **Certain cheeses**: Soft cheeses (such as Camembert and Brie), blue cheeses and any cheeses made using listeria – a type of mould – should be avoided.

- **Raw or undercooked eggs**: Beware the sunny side up! Steer clear of salad cream, egg nog or mayo as these all use raw eggs. Raw or undercooked eggs are a potential source of salmonella food poisoning.

- **Certain fish**: When preparing a fish meal, make sure you avoid shellfish, sushi and, in fact, anything raw or merely 'marinated', such as smoked salmon. Steer clear of shark, swordfish and the more 'exotic' dishes, and even limit the amount of tuna or salmon fish steaks, as they do contain traces of mercury.

- **Rare or medium-rare meat**: Cook meat all the way through to avoid food poisoning, especially those foods such as burgers or lasagne or anything made with minced meat. Always cook pork thoroughly to reduce the chance of trichonosis (worms).

- **Pâté**: Meat or vegetable, because this also contains listeria. Liver-based pâtés also contain high levels of vitamin A. Doctors recommend not to take too much vitamin A as the body cannot process high levels, which could harm the unborn baby.

What to Stock Up on

When preparing meals for the whole family, make sure that you incorporate items recommended during pregnancy as they are good for everyone else too. These foods include:

- **Fruit and vegetables**: Eat plenty of these, including tinned fruit, juices and sauces.

- **Good carbohydrates**: Examples include wholegrain bread, pasta, rice and potatoes.

- **Positive proteins and iron**: Lean meat such as turkey and chicken (avoid fatty meat such as duck), lots of fish, eggs and pulses (beans and lentils).

☑ **Fibre:** Make sure you get plenty of fibre from cereal, wheat products, rice and fresh fruit and vegetables.

☑ **Certain dairy:** Stick to 'good' dairy foods containing calcium for the bones, such as milk, cheese and yoghurt, but beware of the cheeses mentioned earlier!

☑ **Folic acid:** Increase intake of folic acid through foods such as leafy green vegetables and fortified cereals. Liver also contains high levels of folate.

Beware the Calories

Cravings may be king but try to cut down on the chocolate, ice cream, fatty snacks, cakes, biscuits and pies. Swap these for healthier snacks, such as:

☑ **rice cakes**
☑ **malt loaf or fruit bread**
☑ **fresh fruit**
☑ **low-sugar jelly (jello)**
☑ **granola bars**
☑ **home-made popcorn**

Supplements

Many doctors recommend supplementing the nutrients and vitamins that pregnant mothers take in with their food. This can be in the form of tablets or vitamin shakes to build your strength and resistance to colds

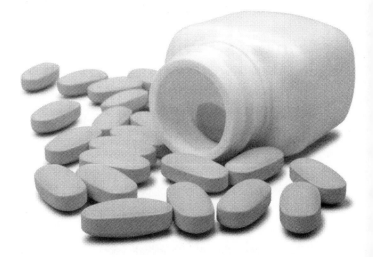

or viruses, and to help protect a woman's bones and body as it undergoes changes. But these can break the budget as they are often high-ticket items. Ways to save can include:

No-frills or own-brand supplements: Look for your store's own-brand vitamin and other supplements as recommended by your doctor. Sometimes supermarkets do vitamin tablets at one-third of the price of your local pharmacy.

 Natural food: Augment your whole family's diet with more natural vitamins and minerals; there are often great bargains to be found on bags of oranges, fruit juices or fresh vegetables, so make the most of these.

Growing Concerns: Feeding Toddlers

A friend once overheard the following comment on a bus, as a young mother scolded her two-year-old, 'No! You're not having your apple until you've eaten your crisps!' It seems that in this instance, the tradition of not eating the sweet until the savoury is finished got in the way of doing what was healthiest. Here are a few reminders about young children's nutritional needs:

Children Need Vitamins and Minerals

If quick snacking for a toddler is usually a bag of crisps or some chocolate, and meals are vitamin-free, something is not right and this will lead to health concerns early on. Without vitamins, their young bodies are susceptible to so many bugs and viruses. Try the following tips:

 Snack substitution: Young children need to eat healthy snacks as well as enjoy the odd treat. Try small packets of raisins, raw carrot sticks, apple slices, grapes, rice cakes, yoghurt or granola.

 Five-a-day: Always include vegetables when making meals. For example, a quick way to do this is to add plum tomatoes, peas or carrots as an accompaniment to something such as fish fingers or sausages. Give them fruit smoothies instead of sugary juice drinks.

Set an example: What you eat, they eat. If your diet is unhealthy, so will theirs be as they will copy your example. Try where you can to have a sit-down meal with them and eat a healthy meal together to get them into good habits.

Protect Their Teeth and Bones

Kids need calcium to grow. But if all they get as meals is breaded chicken drumsticks or chips then they will suffer major health problems. When thinking about the family meal, try the following:

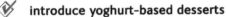

 **swap sugary drinks for milk or flavoured milk**

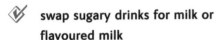 **introduce yoghurt-based desserts**

low-fat flavoured milk can be frozen to make tasty milk 'ice pops'

make up some quick white sauces as an accompaniment to meats

cheesy vegetables will provide calcium *and* vitamins and minerals (do not overdo the cheese)

Trying New Things

Do not despair if they show a violent dislike to broccoli or tomatoes the first time they eat them. Medical research has shown that the taste buds in the under-threes are more sensitive to flavours, especially to new flavours and sensations, than the taste buds of adults. This is why we often hate grapefruit or olives as young children but grow to like them when older. Some tips:

 No pressure: Do not force them to keep eating it, as they will associate the taste with a negative experience.

Be creative: Try to find ways to make it a more enjoyable 'new sensation', such as adding broccoli to cauliflower cheese.

 Reaction not rejection? Be aware that instead of showing a 'dislike' to a food, a toddler might be showing an adverse reaction, so get this checked out medically (and do not just assume it is an intolerance, make *sure* it is one).

Do Not Supersize Them!

They are growing, but they are supposed to grow up, not out. Do not serve them up large helpings at mealtimes. It is good discipline to encourage them to eat as much as they can, but do not force them to eat everything there and then if they are not hungry (their stomachs are much smaller than ours). It can always be saved for later!

Troublesome Teens

It is not easy to cook for teenagers, especially as they will be facing various issues, the least of which will be their lack of desire to sit and eat a family meal with the rest of the household. Teenagers are going through the biggest physical changes of their lives and this will affect the whole family, whether it is an inability to find the floor in their room, suddenly not understanding them any more or the fact that teenagers will eat at different times and need different food – not least good 'brain food' to help them with their studies.

Carbohydrates

Make sure they always have a staple – potatoes, rice, pasta or noodles – as the base for their meal, whether they eat it in their room or in front of the TV or their studies. They need slow-burning, 'good' carbohydrates for energy.

Proteins and Essential Oils

Fresh fish such as tuna, eggs, lean meats such as turkey and chicken or skirt of beef are all important to help them grow into healthy young men and women. Vegetarian and vegan meals can be supplemented by soya, pulses and legumes to help their development. Oily fish are well known for being good 'brain food' due to the essential omega-3 fatty acids (as well as iodine) that they contain, which can help with memory and mental clarity. Omega-3 can also be found in walnut oil and flaxseeds (linseeds).

Five a Day

Teenagers often develop an inability to eat healthily, perhaps because the school does not offer healthy options, or because they do not want their parents to make them a packed lunch any more. So try getting them to take in their essential fresh fruit and veg by:

- incorporating fruit into the breakfast regime – such as fresh figs or grapefruit
- providing fresh juices and smoothies for breakfast and lunch
- using fresh vegetables and salads to accompany their meals
- keeping a fruit bowl in the open – bananas are great football and study fodder
- putting fresh fruit in jelly (jello) or serving it with ice cream
- swapping packaged desserts for watermelon or seasonal fruit salads

Encourage a Family Meal

Even if they are out most of the day and hibernate in their rooms by evening, encourage your teenagers to spend time with the family. Start this habit early and get them involved in the cooking and preparation of family meals. It will be invaluable to your relationships and will also help you to keep an eye on what they are eating. It might even start them talking to you again.

Vegetarians and Vegans

Contrary to popular thought, vegetarianism can be a very healthy way of living, as it cuts out a lot of the fatty meats that other people will eat during a lifetime. But vegetarianism and veganism can be difficult to cater for, and there are certain nutrients and minerals that people who choose not to eat meat or meat products will need to stock up on.

Vegetarians

Most vegetarians do not eat meat primarily on ethical grounds or, in the case of strict Hindus and Buddhists, religious grounds. The obvious foodstuffs that vegetarians usually avoid include all white and red meat, game, reconstituted meats (burgers and sausages, etc.) and fish (though some 'vegetarians' still eat fish). Vegetarians can vary in strictness, however, and many will not consume any food or drink containing elements derived from dead animals, such as meat flavourings (including crisps), certain food colourings (like cochineal, which is derived from the eponymous beetle), anything containing gelatine (which is made from animal protein), cheeses made with calf rennet (as opposed to fungal or bacterial rennet) – and alcohol can contain all kinds of animal derivatives.

Vegans

Vegans have an even stricter diet than vegetarians, as they will avoid all food derived from any kind of exploitation of animals. So in addition to the above, vegans will exclude cheese and dairy food, eggs and honey.

Nutrients That Vegetarians and Vegans Need to Stock Up on

 Vitamin B12: This can be particularly difficult for vegans to get enough of. They should eat plenty of foods containing yeast extract (such as Marmite or Vegemite), fortified bread and fortified breakfast cereals.

 Calcium: As vegans avoid dairy products, they will need to get calcium from food such as kale, soy products and some fortified juices.

Iron: This mineral is primarily found in red meats, so vegetarians and vegans need to eat iron-rich food: pulses; green vegetables such as watercress, broccoli, spring greens and okra; bread and fortified breakfast cereals.

 Protein: This is found in meat and eggs, so people avoiding all animal products should focus on: pulses, nuts and seeds, soya and soya products such as tofu mycoprotein, cereals, bread, rice and maize.

 Selenium: This mineral is prevalent in meat and dairy products, but it is also found in nuts, particularly Brazils.

Diabetes

As you get older, the strain on your body becomes clearer: middle-age spread, a more sedentary lifestyle and the loss of your body's ability to process certain nutrients can all pose a threat to your wellbeing. Think of your family's wider needs: do you have family members in your household who need to cut down on their sugar intake? Do you have a diabetic member of your family? Has your household shopping budget taken into account the needs of those with weight or heart issues?

What Does Diabetes Cause?

For 'type one' and 'type two' diabetes, it is extremely important to control blood sugar levels and blood pressure, to prevent any long-term complications. If it is kept under control, diabetics can live a healthy, normal and active lifestyle. However, poorly controlled diabetes can cause complications such as cardiovascular heart disease, problems with the kidneys, blindness and serious nerve problems that lead to amputation. According to the World Health Organization's survey on the Global Burden of Disease, diabetes is the third most common long-term disease in the UK and the US, after heart disease and cancer.

Types One and Two

 Type one diabetes: This is mostly diagnosed in younger people and develops when the insulin-producing cells in the pancreas are destroyed. This is treated with injections of insulin.

 Type two diabetes: This form is more prevalent among older people and is caused by a resistance to insulin or relatively low insulin levels. It sometimes needs to be treated with medication and insulin injections, but is best treated with good diet and exercise.

What to Eat

Diabetics should try to keep their weight within recommended levels and to eat as healthily as they can. There is nothing they should *never* eat, but just to make sure they eat well. You do not have to eat so-called 'diabetic food', and in fact some doctors recommend that sufferers avoid this. And not buying diabetic food itself helps to keep the household spend lower. However, sufferers should cut down on the amount of fruit juice, which is high in fructose. In addition, think about meals, desserts in particular, and how to prepare food that is low in sugar and low in fat. When planning the family meals, make sure that meals are:

 low in sugar
 low in fat (particularly saturated fat)
 low in salt
 high in fruit and vegetables (at least five portions a day)
 high in starchy carbohydrates (as opposed to sugary carbohydrates) – such as in wholegrain breads and cereal-based food, rice, pasta and potatoes

And try the following:

 fruit bread with low-fat spread

home-made, low-fat crumbles made with less sugar

 unsweetened yoghurt with nuts and fruit

Hypoglycaemia

If a family member is prone to low blood sugar (hypoglycaemia) – which is most commonly linked to diabetes, but can occur as a separate condition – they might sometimes need to increase their blood sugar level quickly, especially if they are out and not near a place to eat. Low blood glucose levels can lead to a variety of symptoms:

 a general sensation of feeling weak

 low energy

 coma

 seizures

 rarely, brain damage or death

What to Do in the Case of an Episode

People who suffer from such episodes should ideally carry glucose tablets (which can be bought over the counter at most pharmacies or food stores), a can of sugary drink or a banana. Where possible, follow this up with something else, such as a sandwich.

Catering for Family Members with Hypoglycaemia

Make sure you factor this into your 'snack' budget when shopping for the family. Also, protect a certain 'store' of snacks solely for the purpose of your family member with low blood sugar levels, and make it clear to other members of the family that this is not for general consumption.

Heart Complaints

Heart disease is the biggest killer in the world. There are two main types of heart disease: coronary (CHD) and cardiovascular (CVD). These can be made much worse, or even caused, by bad diet and no exercise.

Coronary Heart Disease

This is caused when the coronary arteries, which supply the flow of blood to the heart, become narrower due to the build-up of fatty deposits inside them. Eventually, the artery may become so narrow that not enough blood gets through to the heart, the heart muscle does not get the necessary oxygen and the person will suffer from sharp pains, called angina. If the narrowed artery becomes blocked by a blood clot, this causes a heart attack, which can be fatal.

Cardiovascular Disease

Cardiovascular disease includes all diseases of the heart and blood vessels, including heart failure and stroke. It is the world's biggest killer, according to the WHO's 2008 report, *Ten facts on the global burden of disease*. At least 80 per cent of all the fatalities caused by cardiovascular disease globally could have been prevented through healthy eating and a healthy lifestyle, the research claims.

Cut out the Fatty Food!

Fatty, 'convenience' foods may seem cheaper per person, per meal, but as has already been discussed, they work out more expensive in the long term. And, measured against the risk of heart disease, the cost of putting fresh, good produce into your meal plan should seem negligible. Here are ways to cut out the fat while still eating on a budget:

 Cheese: This is a real high-fat food, so start reducing the amount and size of slices you use in meals and sandwiches. You will find the cheese goes a lot further than before, saving you money and protecting your family's waistlines.

Saturated fat: Cut down on your intake of crisps, chips and fries, fried food and ready meals that are high in saturated fat.

 Switch products: Switch from butters to low-fat spreads; from cooking with lard to cooking using unsaturated fat oils, such as sunflower, olive and seed oil.

 Increase vegetable levels: Green vegetables such as spinach and broccoli are good for you. Start swapping greasy, fatty snacks or meal accompaniments such as chips for fresh fruit and vegetables.

Catering for Older Family Members

As you get older, your body needs to supplement its natural defences as one becomes more susceptible to viruses. When thinking about family meals, consider any family members who are older – what sort of food do they need to stock up on? This will help you think about what food you can buy in bulk and at a discount, and how to incorporate this into the meals.

Calcium Counting

Osteoporosis – a condition that affects the bones – is a major health issue for older people, particularly women. This is where bone density reduces and so the risk of fractures increases. Good sources of calcium, which helps to protect and strengthen the bones, are dairy products such as milk, cheese and yoghurt. Points to remember are:

 Watch the fat content: Try to choose lower-fat varieties of dairy products when you can, and provide higher-fat varieties in smaller amounts.

Fish source: Calcium is also found in canned fish with bones, such as sardines.

 Vegetable source: Calcium is also in green leafy vegetables (such as broccoli and cabbage), soya beans and tofu.

Fibre and Starch

As the digestive system slows down with age, it is even more important to help it along with fibre. Food such as bread (wholegrain where possible), cereals, oats, pasta and potatoes are not only low in fat, but high in starchy carbohydrates and fibre, and are also good sources of proteins, some vitamins and minerals. Some fruit, pulses and vegetables are also important sources of fibre.

Iron

The body's store of iron will deplete over time and the older you get, the more iron you will need. The best source of iron is found in red meat – lamb, beef and venison. However, it is also found in pulses, particularly in lentils and peas, oily fish (fresh tuna, for example – tinned tuna is not considered to be an 'oily fish' even if it is canned in oil). You can also get it from eggs, bread, green vegetables and some breakfast cereals. However, watch out for:

 Liver: While liver and kidneys are a good source of iron, meat such as liver is also a rich source of vitamin A, and too much of this in the diet means the body cannot process it all and it builds up. (See below.)

 Caffeine: Drinking too much tea or coffee with iron-rich meals is discouraged by some medical professionals as it could affect the absorption of iron into the body.

Vitamins A, C and D and Folic Acid

These are important for all ages, but particularly to help older family members maintain good health.

- **Vitamin A:** Medical professionals warn that, while small amounts are essential, too much vitamin A (more than 1.5 mg of vitamin A a day, from food and/or supplements) might increase the risk of bone fracture. So, as mentioned above, avoid eating liver or liver products such as pâté more than once a week. If you do eat liver once a week, you should avoid taking any supplements containing vitamin A or fish liver oils (which contain high levels of vitamin A).

- **Vitamin C:** Food containing vitamin C can help the body absorb iron. When planning meals, take into consideration that iron-rich dinners could be accompanied by plenty of vegetables, fruit juice or a dessert incorporating fruit. The best sources of vitamin C are citrus fruit (such as lemons, limes, oranges and grapefruit), as well as green vegetables, bell peppers, tomatoes and even potatoes.

- **Vitamin D:** Like calcium, vitamin D is important for good bone health. We get most of our vitamin D from the effect of sunlight on our skin in the summertime, but vitamin D is also found in oily fish and eggs, as well as foods with added vitamins such as some breakfast cereals and margarines.

- **Folic acid:** Good sources are green vegetables and brown rice, as well as bread and breakfast cereals, particularly those which have added vitamins.

Cater for the Right Portions

As people get older, they tend to need to eat less, owing to the less physically active lifestyle. So do not serve up large portions at family meal times that the older members either cannot tolerate, or that will go to waste. Serve smaller meals, more regularly, and make sure there are some healthy snacks available.

Blood Pressure

Salt in Small Doses

On average, you should aim to keep your salt intake to less than 6 g per day as it can have a bad effect on blood pressure. This is not easy, as most of the salt we eat is already in food. Therefore, it is important to be aware of the salt content of ready-prepared foods and avoid adding salt to your food when cooking and at the table.

Positive Potassium

Potassium, however, has a beneficial effect on blood pressure, helping to lower it and reduce the risk of heart-related problems. Fruit and vegetables such as bananas, tomatoes and avocados are good sources of potassium.

Protecting Your Family and the Budget

It is not easy to cater for all these different health requirements. And it can be expensive if you do not have the right tools to help you. But if you think laterally, you will find ways to cut down on expenditure and wastage, and help protect your family's health and wealth in these difficult times.

Avoiding Waste

Wasting food is the biggest thing that will affect your budget. If you make sure that you are catering accordingly for each person's needs, however, then you will be serving the right portions, not more, and buying the right food, not stuff that cannot be eaten and will only get wasted in the end.

Start Collecting 'Healthy' Recipes

There are many healthy recipes in this book (*see pages 174–253*) to get you started – and they are geared towards protecting your budget as well! Once you are on your way, you can always:

Share and care: Ask around and share recipes with your friends and colleagues; they might know where some good deals are to be had on special food.

Ask the experts: Consult your doctor or nutritionist for a list of recommended food for the family.

Website watch: Even if you are not a member (and adding membership fees to your budget is not the aim of this guide), sites such as www.weightwatchers.com can help you think about cooking your way to a better, healthier family. And you can find all sorts of recipes on the web.

The Family Kitchen

PACKED WITH
MONEY
SAVING
IDEAS & TIPS

Creating Meals

With most families finding that they need two salaries to live on in these credit-crunch times, it is becoming more of a chore to think about cooking a meal every night. It is no surprise that many people opt for the takeaway, ready meal or the convenience store for the nightly dinner. Plus, with many families working on shift patterns, teenagers out or hibernating in their rooms for much of the evening, planning and preparing the family meal can be almost impossible. Almost, but not quite.

Working out Quantities

Singledom is the best time to learn to cook, but it cannot prepare you for the onslaught of getting family meals ready each day. Even assuming that everyone in the house likes and can eat the same food (which would be a miracle), the sheer quantities of food involved can be mind-boggling.

Cooking with Bulk Items

Having saved money in buying family-sized packs or bulk items such as noodles, frozen peas or rice, it is sometimes tempting to use a little more of these than we should in each meal, because the bag or packet looks never-ending. Here is a secret – it is not. It will run out sooner than you think, unless you are careful.

Don't Just Use it Up

If you think there is only a little bit of a certain ingredient left, you might be tempted to throw it all in. Don't. It will only get wasted. Try making it into something, such as a soup or stuffing.

Never Over-estimate

Too often we are not convinced a certain amount of food will be enough per person. But think about the various appetites: small children and older people will not eat huge portions. Try the following:

- ✅ **Measure it out!** Until you get used to cooking a certain dish so that you can automatically gauge the right amount, use measuring cups, scales and jugs to help you get the right portion per person.

- ✅ **Make a fist**: This should be the size of a portion of noodles, mashed potato or rice to accompany a meal.

- ✅ **Count the carrots**: Assume, as a rough rule of thumb, that half a carrot should be apportioned per person as part of a wider meal. Apply the same rule to parsnips, celery, courgettes (zucchini) and aubergines (eggplant).

- ✅ **Divvy up the potatoes**: When doing roasts, count the prepared potatoes in the pan and allocate a certain even number to each person (usually between four and six). Someone will always want more or less so it balances out.

Working from Recipes

This is the easiest way to gauge how much food you will need to prepare per person. Recipes enable you to:

- ✅ **Plan the shop**: Do you need more chicken than you have in the freezer for instance?

- ✅ **Conduct mental swaps**: Work out what to replace certain ingredients with so that you can use what you have, rather than buy new ones.

- ✅ **Think about portion allocation**: Estimate how much each family member can eat.

Think about leftovers: You will be able to gauge whether you will have enough left over for someone's lunch the next day.

Trial and Error

If you are not working from a recipe, or the recipe resulted in too much or too little, you will learn from trial and error: if you have not baked enough lasagne one day, for example, make a note of it and increase the amounts you use the next time; if you have made too much food, write down what tends to get half-eaten or left on plates and cook less of it next time.

Time Matters

It is no wonder people grab a takeaway, open a ready-made pasta packet or bung a ready meal into the microwave. We live in a fast-paced world and while we might enjoy cooking when there is time, we often find ourselves pressed for time: work, family, other commitments all crowd in. But it *is* possible to stop buying the convenience food and the ready-made sauces and start saving money while not adding to our stress levels.

The Kitchen Time Lord

Students eating at weird hours of the day, working adults coming home late and children leaving school early and demanding to be fed immediately: all these can take the stuffing out of the person preparing the food. And if we are not careful, this will take the stuffing out of our budget as well. So try not to keep people waiting too long for their meal or they will snack, but also remember to work in small stages so you do not have to do many things at once.

A Step in Time

Knowing in advance when people will get up and come back home is a starting point. Of course, this involves communication, but preparing home-cooked meals and snacks will save lots of money, helping the family not to rely on takeaways or quick-fix ready meals, while getting them involved, however old they are. If you can achieve this communication, it can help in the following ways:

After breakfast:

- put the meat in the fridge to defrost
- get the family to help lay the table for lunch/dinner
- prepare ingredients for the main meal (carrots can be peeled in advance, for example)
- prepare a light snack for whoever will be home earlier (if it is not you)

In the evening:

- give the light snack to the early returners
- finish the preparation
- cook the meal
- get family to help clear up as you go along, or stir things
- when serving up, leave enough aside covered in a Pyrex dish for latecomers
- put this into a plate-warmer/the still-warm oven if they are on their way
- if very late, latecomers can warm up their meal in the microwave/slow cooker
- before latecomers return, get the family to help you clear away
- freeze any leftovers

Keep it Simple

Everyone wants the cooking to be appreciated by those who eat it, but it can be very stressful, not least because of the time a big meal such as a roast dinner may take to prepare and cook. If you are cooking a 'big' meal for the whole family to sit down to at the same time, you can minimize your preparation and cooking time. Here is how:

Limit the Ingredients

If you are going to cook a casserole, why complicate it with by lots of vegetables to the casserole as well as having vegetable accompaniments? Add maybe one or two to the casserole and just have potatoes and peas on the side. It saves you much peeling and chopping that way.

Limit the Cooking Stages

Why make extra work for yourself? For example, a quick cheat's Carbonara will not involve fussing around with eggs, but using a quick white cheese sauce instead. When baking a cake, do all the mixing in a saucepan after melting the butter and sugar in the saucepan first, then taking it off the heat.

Multi-task

Save yourself time by doing some preparation at the same time as something else: peel the vegetables the night before while watching TV with the family, or while you are on the phone.

Cheat!

Ready-roll icing, just-roll pastry and cookie dough straight from the freezer – we have all done it and, if it saves time and stress, it can be worth paying for it. Making pastry from scratch but doing it wrong is even more costly....

Ask for Help

Do not be a kitchen martyr. Get the family to help, either in laying the table or making the sauce or peeling and chopping.

Getting the Family Involved

The last point above, asking for help, is perhaps something many families do not do, assuming that perhaps the children are too young to do anything to help, or sticking to stereotyped male and female roles about whose kitchen it is anyway. But if you want to stick to a family budget, you should stick to having a family kitchen – which means getting them all involved in various ways.

The Youngest Members

Children of all ages love to cook and there are many things they can do to help out around the kitchen. These include:

- **Cereal cakes**: Stirring cereal into melted chocolate and making a mess, that is to say, snacks for the whole family to enjoy.

- **Laying the table**: Even the smallest children can do this, although an adult or older child should take responsibility for knives and forks.

- **Clearing away**: Teach them how to properly clean and stack plates at the end of the meal (so there are no nasty bits of food sticking to the bottoms of plates!).

- **Condiments**: They can take condiments from the fridge to the table.

- **Stirring cold things**: Only the older children, that is, teenagers, should stir hot (and so potentially scalding) liquids or food.

- **Filling pies**: Spooning pie filling into pre-made or shop-bought crusts is fun and easy.

- **Cakes**: Young children can help to make cakes by stirring while you add flour, and decorating them.

Older Children

Older children and young teens can make their own cakes using recipes adapted for young people; they can take more responsibility for washing up or laying the table; they are old enough to be able to stir or watch over hot pots on the stove; and they are old enough to be trusted to peel and, for older teens, to chop vegetables and fruit. Even teenage boys can peel potatoes before soccer practice....

Adults

The older folks can be the best or the worst people to have around as everyone is suddenly an expert in the kitchen and wants to tell you how it should be done. Unless they are brilliant cooks and work well together with you, and you trust them to get on with doing part of the meal themselves, then ways to make older folk feel included and help you (without sending your stress levels sky high) are:

- **Dessert duty:** Get them to make part of the dessert, such as do the custard for a trifle, or prepare the fruit for a crumble.

- **Salad duty:** Put them on salad duty, which is a nicely separate element of the meal for them to concentrate on.

- **Chopping duty:** Ask them to chop the vegetables.

- **More use elsewhere?** Send them out of the kitchen to find some good wine to have with the meal or keep an eye on the children.

Rotas

Adult children and other family members over the age of 18 are all capable of doing something and, if they follow a set plan and recipe, they should be able to make the meal themselves. Why not set a rota to help give the main meal-maker a night or two off each week?

Bringing the Family on Board

As the family budget is being trimmed to cater for these difficult economic times, it is important that the focus is on what the family would like and how to get them all to participate in saving money and making their own meals. Try to get them thinking:

- **Meal plans**: Involve the family with the meal plan at the start of the week and encourage them to come up with their own ideas for dinners. Make lists of easy meals that they can make or prepare.

- **Money-saving education**: Suggest ways that they can help save money when shopping and get them to think of ways to eat healthily without spending more money. Teach them the importance of not wasting food.

- **Show them the results**: Make sure they actually see what savings are made or the number of lunches achieved by clever cooking and planning ahead.

Plan Your Weekly Meals in Advance

It sounds counter-intuitive, but many time-pressed families like to plan their meals a few days ahead. Of course, there are days when you just cannot summon the energy to cook or even think about what to rustle up. And trying to get children to wash, dress and eat before school can be more of a battle than a breeze. But leaving everything to the last minute can sometimes involve spending on takeaways, resorting to easy, sugary breakfast items or rushing out after work to buy a 'missing ingredient' instead of having the luxury of time to find a bargain.

Planning Pays

Making a mental note as to what to cook through the week has several advantages:

Interest: You can plan a varied menu to avoid boredom, and if you get your family involved they might even get excited about planning the meals.

Wellbeing: You can introduce more healthy options to your meals and it will reduce your stress levels to know everything you need is already in the house and ready to use.

Better quality: Thinking about food in advance means you do not have to rely on convenience foods.

Better price: Working out what you want to eat means you can think about where the bargains or special offers are to be found on healthier items.

Think of the Store Cupboard When You Are Shopping

There is a lot to be said for planning meals or working out where the bargains are to be found, but it is also worthwhile stocking up on your staples and long-life ingredients, especially when these are on special offer or you can buy in bulk. Examples of store-cupboard staples are: rice, lentils, vinegar, oils, sauces, flour, pasta, tins of chopped or plum tomatoes, and so on. We will look at store-cupboard essentials later on (*see page 151*). As well as saving money on offers or bulk buying, if you keep a stocked cupboard, you need never worry about not having anything in to eat. Of course, if you have any students in the house who will not cook, then they will still complain, but they will soon learn that it takes no time at all to boil a little pasta and toss it afterwards with a dash of oil, while making a sauce from a tin of plum tomatoes, a chopped onion, some herbs and a splash of Worcestershire sauce. This should satisfy any student's craving for eight meals a day.

Shopping List for a Week of Family Meals

An example shopping list for a week of four-person family meals could be as follows. This does not take into account breakfast or lunch, but does assume that you have to buy some store-cupboard/longer-life fridge items such as herbs, sugar, eggs, margarine or rice from scratch. You may need to substitute the meat for vegetarian options (such as soya-based substitutes).

- meat joint or whole chicken (from butcher)
- minced/ground beef
- chicken pieces (family pack, frozen, breaded)
- carrots (big no-frills or basics bag)
- potatoes (big no-frills or basics bag, suitable for baking or roasting)
- bag of onions
- peas (big freezer bag)
- courgettes/zucchini (several)
- bananas
- bag of oranges
- apples (big no-frills or basics bag)
- 1 lettuce
- fresh tomatoes
- 1 cucumber
- milk (5 l/8½ pts/5 qts)
- cheese
- low-fat family-size spread
- butter
- ice cream
- yoghurts (pick them up on two-for-one!)
- pot of custard powder
- lasagne sheets (basics range)
- big bag of pasta shapes
- big bag of rice
- tinned tuna (4–6-pack)
- tinned sweetcorn (4–6-pack)
- canned tomatoes (4–6-pack)
- juice (4 l/1 gal/4 qts)
- eggs (12-pack)
- Italian dried herbs

nutmeg
 flour
 bread (wholegrain if possible)
 cooking oil

Example Weekly Meal Plan

This takes into account leftovers and food that can be frozen. It does not take into account breakfast or lunch, except where stated.

 Sunday: For lunch or dinner: a meat roast, with potatoes, carrots, broccoli, peas, stuffing* and gravy*. For dessert: apple crumble* and ice-cream.

 Monday: For lunch: cold meat and stuffing sandwiches*. For dinner: tuna and sweetcorn pasta bake (using two tins of tuna and two of sweetcorn); salad, if needed (lettuce, cucumber, tomatoes). For dessert: stewed apples* or bananas and custard*.

 Tuesday: For dinner: large lasagne* with béchamel* and meat sauces, and salad (lettuce, cucumber, tomatoes) or vegetables. For dessert: yoghurt and shortbread biscuits*.

 Wednesday: For breakfast: rest of the yoghurt. For lunch: any of the lasagne left over. For dinner: baked potatoes with anything (tuna, sweetcorn, grated carrot, cheese, any remaining salad). For dessert: home-made banana cake*.

 Thursday: For breakfast: leftover bananas not used for the dessert on Wednesday. For dinner: chicken pieces with rice and peas (you can bread the chicken pieces, or cook them in a sauce using remaining tinned tomatoes, onions and herbs). For dessert: glazed oranges with ice cream (slice the oranges, heat them in a frying pan and glaze with sugar caramelized in a pan).

☑ **Friday:** For breakfast: leftover pieces of orange not used for the dessert on Thursday. For lunch: any remaining chicken pieces in sauce with rice. For dinner: fishcakes* with vegetables – peas, carrots or, if there is any minced meat/soya left, a chilli con carne*. For dessert: pancakes* with any leftover ice cream, sugar or fruit.

☑ **Saturday:** For dinner or lunch: create a kedgeree, risotto or paella with any remaining vegetables, such as courgettes, tomatoes, peas, cheese. For dessert: finish the banana cake – you deserve it – and the shopping round begins again.

*What You Did Not Buy Because You Made it Yourself

Avoid buying many items ready-made, as your costs will escalate. There are so many elements to the meals above that you can easily make from the few things you have bought or already have in the store cupboard (*see pages 147–163 for some more hints about how to make these*):

☑ **Gravy and stuffing:** You made some gravy from the meat juices and some flour. See page 141 for a stuffing recipe.

☑ **Apple crumble:** You stewed the apples and made the crumble from the butter, flour and sugar.

☑ **Béchamel sauce:** You used flour, low-fat spread, milk and nutmeg.

☑ **Pasta sauce:** You made it from the tinned tomatoes, herbs and minced/ground meat.

☑ **Custard:** You may not have literally made this from scratch, but you made it up from the powder, sugar and milk, rather than buying ready-made, perishable custard.

☑ **Shortbread biscuits:** You made them from flour, butter and sugar.

☑ **Pancakes:** You made them from flour, eggs, milk and butter.

- **Chilli con carne:** You made it with onions, minced meat, any tomatoes and sweetcorn (or kidney beans if you had them!).

- **Fishcakes:** You used up any tuna, sweetcorn and herbs with the potatoes.

- **Banana cake:** You made this with flour, butter, sugar, eggs and bananas.

- **Breaded chicken pieces**: Made using herbs, dried breadcrumbs and egg.

- **Lasagne:** No need to buy frozen or ready-made; you made it from scratch as described.

What is Left Over?

The juices and milks should just last the whole week, and most of the fresh fruit, vegetables and meat will be used up early on, but reused once cooked to avoid wastage. However, there will be some things which have still not been used, and this can save you money on the next shop as you will not have to restock certain items:

- **staples like rice and pasta if you bought a lot in bulk**
- **flour and sugar can last a long while**
- **herbs and spices can keep for over a year**
- **cooking oil keeps for ages as well**
- **portions of leftovers, and whole dishes, in the freezer**

Catering for Differing Appetites

Even if the whole family is on board and willing to help, there is always the fact that we all have our likes and dislikes. Think about ordering a pizza – no two people will agree on toppings. It is the same thing with making dinner for several people. Sometimes, two different meals may have to be made, especially when catering for vegetarians or vegans. This can cause friction between families and often results in a bigger food expenditure as busy people often just buy two lots of food items to minimize the stress of thinking ahead.

This Is Where the Plan Comes into its Own

This is all about planning, whether setting the budget or making the list or thinking of the food for the week ahead. With a weekly plan, the whole family can see what the meals are, what options may be open to them and you can think in advance where you might need to adjust the menu or buy a certain ingredient (such as tofu) instead of meat.

Allergies and Intolerances

Cater for these in your weekly plan and make sure the other family members do not tease or make the sufferer feel excluded from family meals. Where possible, find some common ground via which you can all eat together.

Compromise

If someone does not like a particular ingredient, but other family members do, this does not have to become a bone of contention or mean that you bust your budget.

- **Find something the whole family enjoys**: If they all like spaghetti carbonara with ham and mushrooms, except that one person hates mushrooms, either serve it without or take the mushrooms out of his or her serving.

- **Agree to ditch an ingredient**: Taking out an offensive ingredient such as mushrooms is one thing, but what if it is something that really permeates the whole dish, such as garlic? If people really cannot eat something that tastes or smells even a little of garlic, then take it out of the family food shop. You can still eat garlicky food when you are out in a restaurant or if that family member is away.

- **Majority rule**: If 50 per cent of the family wants one thing and 50 per cent another, then it is worth changing the menu to something they can agree on. But if every member except one person wants a certain meal, then suggest an alternative for that person, and base this on something you already have in your fridge or freezer – do not go out especially or cook something new from scratch.

WWVD?

What would vegetarians do? What do vegans eat? Pretty much anything, apart from meat and meat by-products. So when thinking about the family meal, you might sometimes consider the following:

Everyone goes veggie: Get everyone to all 'go vegan' for certain meals and enjoy a nice saag aloo (spinach and tofu) with rice or a delicious pasta with cherry tomatoes and avocado.

Get inspiration: Invest in a couple of vegetarian or vegan recipe books.

Sauces: Making sauces without meat for various dishes is not that difficult; you can always add meat to a separate dish for the omnivores.

Anticipation: Make extra of a vegetable dish such as curry or vegetable pie and freeze it for a future occasion when everyone else may be eating a meat dish.

It Is a Balancing Act

You are never going to please all the people all the time. You will not even be able to feed all of the people all at the same time. But with a little preparation and encouragement to get the whole family on board, you can all work together to help reduce the household spend on food, minimize wastage and cut back on extra expenditure on easy convenience food. And if it teaches others how to cook for themselves, or fosters greater understanding of all the different pressures in providing a family meal on a tight budget, then this will be a valuable lesson for future generations to learn. Some useful websites are:

 www.vegansociety.com
 www.cookingforvegans.co.uk
 www.cookerycircle.co.uk
 www.netmums.com

The Cheap Meal Challenge

In the UK, a national supermarket chain has been advertising ways that a family of four can cook a meal for just £5 ($7). But even if this can be done, can it include extras such as dessert? Does it have to be completely done from scratch? And can families buy food for the week and generate interesting meals each day, without resorting to the seemingly cheap yet very unhealthy option of opening a couple of pizza boxes?

The Simple Answer...

....is yes. It can include desserts (see the case study on the Appleyards at the end of this section), it does not always have to be done from scratch each time and it is not difficult for families to budget for a series of interesting meals that do not require a huge number of ingredients.

Mix and Match

We have already seen a weekly menu plan and corresponding shopping list in 'Creating Meals'. But let us explore in more detail exactly how to:

- use and reuse ingredients
- 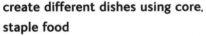 create different dishes using core, staple food
- find cheap cuts of meat and fish and cook them

Versatile Ingredients

When buying and planning the meals, always think about food that can be used in several different ways. This will help you if you want to buy in bulk – how many dishes can you create using that one bulk packet of a certain food item? Thinking about the versatility of ingredients can really help you cut back on the number of different food items that you buy, which will reduce your budget significantly.

Versatile Staples

If you have a range of basic staple ingredients, you can chop and change and be prepared to be as flexible as possible within given time limits. Staples can be used in the following ways:

- **Rice:** In addition to using it as a plain accompaniment to curries or stews, you can cook kedgeree, risotto, paella, rice pudding and egg-fried rice, or use it in rissoles, stuffing, soups, stews and casseroles, or prepare it with fish or vegetables for a salad.

- **Potatoes:** Mash them, boil them, fry them into chips and fries, bake them into wedges, puree them to form the basis of a thick soup, chunk them into curries, casseroles and stews, roast them, make them into fishcakes, bubble 'n' squeak, moussaka, shepherd's pie, fish pie, hash browns, potato salad or the standard baked potato.

- **Noodles:** Use noodles in stir-fries and soups, as ramen-style noodles, egg-fried noodles, or plain noodles to accompany another dish.

- **Pasta (shapes, not ravioli, cannelloni, tortellini or spaghetti):** Eat pasta freshly cooked and tossed in a sauce or accompanying 'meat and two veg', or make macaroni cheese, macaroni milk pudding, pasta bakes or pasta salad, or put pasta in soups and stews (such as minestrone soup).

Versatile Meat

There is more to meat than a roast dinner or bangers and mash. We will come on to the different fresh meat cuts that you can get to suit every type of budget, but let us look at ways of using variations on the meat theme, taking some of the cheapest available meat products:

- **Burger meat:** Available in big freezer packs and often at a discount, it is tempting just to slap these between two slices of bread roll with some cheese and bacon. However, these can also be used to make stews, hearty soups, casseroles, patties and pies and pasta sauces (if cooked and broken up with some onion, herbs and chopped tomatoes).

- **Minced/ground meat:** This can be used to make various bulk meals that can be stored and frozen for future use. Some of its uses include bubble 'n' squeak, chilli con carne, lasagne, meatloaf, meatballs, pasta sauce, pies and patties, rissoles, shepherd's pie, cottage pie and meat timbales.

- **Tinned meat:** This includes tinned ham, spam and that other staple from the Second World War, corned beef. Ways to use these include bubble 'n' squeak, cold sandwiches, cold as part of a ploughman's lunch, hot sandwiches such as melts, shepherd's pie, pastries, rissoles, sliced into salads, in pasta dishes (tinned ham, cut into chunks) and in soups.

- **Sandwich (sliced, packaged) meat:** This does not just have to be put into sandwiches. It can also be used in the following ways: in hot melts, added to pizza topping, eaten cold as part of a ploughman's or other light lunch, salads (sliced thinly), mixed into pasta dishes such as carbonara, pastries and *croque monsieurs/madames*.

Sausages: Delightful hot or cold, on their own or inside a roll or sandwich, they can also be used in a sausage and pepper casserole; cooked, sliced and added to beans; diced up in a lasagne; cut up into chunks and added to stews; served cold, sliced, with salad; or in pastries.

Fishy Tales

Whether you get your fish right from the wharf, out of a tin or a cut from the supermarket, you can cook it many ways. Some of these methods can create a big quantity of food for a small amount of money. These dishes can then be put into the freezer to save for another day. Ways to cook or use fish (tinned, frozen or fresh) include: cold inside sandwiches (tinned) or as a filling for baked potatoes; in curries, kedgerees, paellas, fish chowders, roulades, fisherman's pie, pasta bakes, pastries, mousses, kebabs or warm salads; baked, poached, grilled/broiled, fried (with or without batter), mashed with potatoes to make fishcakes, pickled or breadcrumbed; or eaten on their own, accompanied by rice or salad and bread.

Vegetable Delights

It is surprising how many ways vegetables can be used, when they are usually thought of as accompaniments to the meat-and-potatoes section of a meal. You can use vegetables in pasta dishes, curries, lasagnes, kebabs, pies, pastries, rice dishes, stir-fries, casseroles, stews, soups and salads. You can serve them roasted, baked (half an aubergine/eggplant can be halved, hollowed out, mixed with tomatoes and onion and refilled, then baked with cheese, for example), stuffed (peppers for instance), barbecued, grilled within hot melts, made into vegetarian burgers and sausages or, of course, raw.

Cheap Cuts of Meat

One student from Australia claimed that meat is just too expensive to be part of the diet for someone living on a tight budget. But this is not actually the case. What is true is that people used to going to the supermarket to buy their meat will only be presented with the prices on the counter. More than that, they will only be offered meat from a limited selection of cuts and produce. This gives the false impression that meat is too expensive to be able to be part of a 'cheap meal challenge'.

Think Continental

Speaking to a Hungarian gentleman of advanced years, he proclaimed, 'I don't understand why young families these days say they cannot afford meat. We escaped from Hungary with nothing but the clothes on our backs and yet always ate well. But you Anglo-Saxons don't know about cheap cuts of meat.' Well, that is not entirely true. We do, or we did during the war years, but most of us have forgotten what these cuts are. Well, cheap cuts of meat include:

- ☑ **cheeks**
- ☑ **trotter**
- ☑ **liver**
- ☑ **hock**
- ☑ **shoulder**
- ☑ **chump**
- ☑ **oxtail**
- ☑ **skirt**
- ☑ **brisket**
- ☑ **tongue (technically offal – see below)**

Where Do You Get These?

These are all available at butchers and markets, particularly specialist meat markets. You can also buy some of them from the fresh meat sections of the larger superstores, although the variety will be restricted and you will be paying retail, not wholesale, prices.

How to Cook Cheap Cuts of Meat

The cheap cuts of meat are often less expensive because they tend to be tougher than the usual cuts such as t-bone or rib-eye. But they are also lean (less fatty) and, with the right treatment, are extremely tasty. Some suggestions include:

Cheeks: Beef cheeks are gaining in popularity in top restaurants, particularly as business people are reducing their entertainment budgets and exploring different options. Try slow-cooking beef cheeks in some red wine or a treacle and vinegar sauce for a few hours until tender. Serve hot in its juices with some creamy mash, roast parsnips and hot English mustard.

Oxtail: This is the tail of a steer or cow and is notoriously tough. Tenderize it and slow-cook it in a meaty broth until the juices permeate the liquid. Cut away the meat and boil it up in a stew, together with chunks of carrot, leeks and turnip or swede. Serve on its own or with baby new potatoes.

Skirt: This is the underpart, or belly, of a cow or lamb. This is a very lean meat and can take up to 6 hours until it is tender enough to eat. Tenderize it and put this in a slow-cooker or hay box along with some stock and chopped vegetables. When you get home, add some fresh dumplings and serve.

Tongue: Although technically offal, this is a delicious meat and can be bought very cheaply. It is also versatile, and can be used, when cold, as sandwich filling: take some ciabatta, onion relish and some salad leaves and provide yourself with a top-quality meat sandwich.

Offal

This is basically everything else left over when the main flesh has been taken from the carcass of an animal – it includes the entrails and organs. Dishes using offal were very popular even 40 years ago and were often sold as basic pub grub alongside the traditional steak and chips. However, there are various reasons why offal has lost its popularity, not least because of the meat scares of the 1990s, with CJD, the human variant of BSE and scrapie, meaning that people shunned meat, and are only just starting to come back to it but do not feel brave enough to deal with offal. Also, of course, there is the squeamish factor involved with buying and cooking and, for some, the knowledge that you could be eating one of the following:

- head
- brain
- brawn (or 'head cheese' – meat from an animal's head, set in its gelatine, with onion and seasoning)
- snout
- tongue
- chitterlings (pig's intestine)
- tripe (the stomach from a milk-fed calf)
- giblets (various organs from fowl, used in gravies and stews)
- heart
- kidneys
- lungs (called the lights)
- liver
- sweetbreads (the thymus glands or the pancreas)
- fries (the testicles)
- scrotum (yummy)
- chickens' feet (a delicacy in Peruvian soups)
- trotters

I Would Never Eat Those!

But you eat sausages, haggis, re-formed meat burgers (what do you think they use to make them?). You might like to eat steak and kidney pie or liver as part of a mixed grill. You may have eaten Scrapple sandwiches in the States (which is meat made from a combination of pig offal) and maybe munched through some Rocky Mountain Oysters, which are bulls' testes. Moreover, if you have eaten some of these things, you probably really enjoyed them.

Ways to Make Offal Delicious

Many of the following suggestions are delicious. What is more, the ingredients are really cheap to buy and will fit well within your 'cheap meal challenge' budget. Just do not tell the kids what they are eating.

Stuffed Heart

This delicacy was very popular until the 1980s, a time of wide shoulder pads, giant hair and a sense of wealth that saw cheap meats being kicked off the menu. Here is an ancient recipe dating back to early medieval France:

- 1 beef or ox heart (about 1.4 kg/3 lb)
- 150 g/5 oz/3⅓ cups parsley, finely chopped
- 1 sprig coriander/cilantro, finely chopped
- 2 tsp thyme leaves, chopped
- 1 tsp rosemary, chopped
- 3 tbsp butter
- 120 ml/4 fl oz/½ cup red wine
- 120 ml/4 fl oz/½ cup water
- salt and black pepper, to taste
- flour, for sprinkling
- 50 ml/2 fl oz/¼ cup redcurrant jam/jelly
- 50 ml/2 fl oz/¼ cup cream or milk
- freshly cooked mashed potato, to serve
- freshly cooked runner beans, to serve

Halve the heart lengthways and remove any fat, arteries, blood and sinew, then pat dry. Cream the butter and blend well with all the herbs. Stuff the heart with the herb mixture then tie it into a roll with butchers' string. Sprinkle with flour and brown it in melted butter in a deep frying pan or large saucepan.

Once the heart has coloured nicely, add the red wine and water to the pan and season well. Cover and allow to simmer for about 3 hours, turning occasionally (add some stock or more water if it becomes too dry). You can also do this in a lidded casserole dish, placed in an oven preheated to about 150°C/300°F/Gas Mark 2). When the heart is tender, remove the meat from the pan and set aside to keep warm. Make a gravy by adding 1–2 tbsp flour to the pan juices and then stirring in the redcurrant jam, followed by the cream or milk. Slice the meat and serve on a bed of mashed potato with runner beans and gravy.

Lovely Liver

Too often, liver reminds us of school dinners, of a grey and flabby meat that tasted very strongly of iron. Schools bought it because it was cheap. But although it is cheap, it can be done beautifully. Buy it fresh and grill it well with some salt, pepper and a dash of barbecue sauce. Fry some bacon and layer it on top of the liver. Balance on a bed of creamy mashed potato and serve with generous lashings of thick red wine gravy.

Sweetbreads

These are the thymus gland (which comes in two parts, hence the plural) or, occasionally, the pancreas. The most desirable cut is the heart thymus, rather than the throat thymus, which can be tough and less tasty. They are a delicate, silky meat, usually white or slightly pink. If they are red, it means the animal was older (and the sweetbreads will not be so tasty).

Preparation: Usually best within 24 hours of buying, they should be prepared well, as raw sweetbreads often have a layer of fat and a sinewy outer membrane that must be peeled away first. You can soak sweetbreads in white wine or vinegar for several hours, changing the liquid a couple of times. This makes it easier to remove the membrane and 'clean' the meat. After washing, they can be breaded and deep-fried, grilled or barbecued, and added to fresh, crunchy salad.

Other Dishes

In addition to the above, there are many other dishes you can make very cheaply, some of which will stretch a long way. These include:

- steak and kidney pie
- giblet and sweetcorn soup
- haggis
- pâté
- breaded chitterlings with chips/fries and peas
- pigs' trotters with butter beans
- breaded herby tripe with braised cabbage and sweet parsnip mash

Don't Knock It 'til You've Tried It

You may be thinking that some of this sounds a little bit too much like *The Silence of the Lambs*, but it has really only been about 20 years since people stopped buying and eating offal regularly. It is coming back into fashion among the business classes and so prices are starting to rise slightly, but it is still cheap and if you are prepared to try a few easy recipes, you will find the whole family can enjoy eating meat regularly even on a tight budget.

Making Impressive Fish Dishes Cheaply

Fish is generally much cheaper than its meaty counterpart, and you can get many frozen cuts of fish for low prices. But you do not need to pay through the nose for fresh fish steaks or whole fish, and the taste difference between fresh fish and frozen can be marked.

Look for the No-brand Cuts

Basics or value cuts of fish such as tuna steak or salmon may not have the same taste assurance as luxury brand or well-known producers. But if you are looking for something that will be used as part of another dish, or poached with plenty of flavourings, then it is worth buying the basics.

Whole Fish

These can be bought straight from the wharf at salesman's prices, and you can guarantee their freshness. But you can also get great fish from specialist markets, where you can buy in bulk, take home and freeze yourself, or from your local fishmonger.

Small is Beautiful

For a cheap fish meal, do not go to the local fish and chip shop. Instead, buy small, fresh sardines (which can work out more expensive than a tin, but which will be much larger and therefore more cost-effective). Clean them, lightly fry them in some oil and dried dill, then dip them in a mixture of dill, breadcrumbs and egg. Fry them up again lightly whole for a delicious, crispy and posh-looking meal, accompanied by minted peas and floury new potatoes.

The Cod Alternative

Cod is becoming over-fished and so is in danger of becoming a 'watched' species on environmental groups' list of various species. Thus, its increasing scarcity means that prices are soaring sky-high. This can be seen in the supermarket shelves or on the menu, with cod fillets costing almost as much as some tuna or salmon steaks. But you can use similarly flavoured and textured white fish to create just as tasty meals as you would with cod, such as the lovely chilli fishcakes suggested here:

Rock Cakes with Chilli Sauce: Rock is a slightly more fishy-tasting cod variant, but it is half the price of cod. Lightly cook this fish until it flakes well when touched with a fork, then mash it up together with some fresh dill, a squeeze of lemon, egg white and some finely diced pre-cooked potatoes; add some dried chilli powder to the mixture, pat it into small cakes, then fry them in a shallow pan with some oil for 3–5 minutes, turning until golden brown on both sides; serve at once with some roast cherry tomatoes and some sweet chilli sauce (home-made is best, but shop-bought will do as this keeps for a long time).

From Smoked Salmon to Gravadlax

If you want a dish to impress, starting off with smoked salmon never goes amiss. But it is often far too expensive for the average person's food budget. Gravadlax is a cheaper variation on the theme.

 To make Gravadlax: Buy a decent-sized, middle cut of salmon from your local fishmonger and remove the backbone from the fish, which should give you two fillets; place one fillet in a dish, covering it with dill, a squeeze of lemon, 2 teaspoons brandy, 2 tablespoons caster/superfine sugar, 2 tablespoons sea salt and plenty of crushed black peppercorns; place the second fillet on top, with the skin facing outwards, cover with kitchen foil and put something heavy on top, such as a frying pan; refrigerate for 3–4 days, turning and basting twice a day; rinse, then dry it out, slice thinly and serve.

A Last Word

There are so many ways to make a cheap meal that can include meat in various forms and fresh fish. You do not have to resort to bargain basement packets of burgers and fish fingers. When thinking about your own family's cheap meal challenge, try going beyond the boundaries of what you have been used to, or the 'easy' options presented by the supermarkets. The more you can cook these dishes, the more varied the menu will become, all the while sticking to your budget – and even cutting your budget further.

Case Study: The Appleyards

Christopher and Rhian Appleyard, from Surrey, UK, and their student children Rachel (21) and Richard (19) tried the taste challenge. They found that they could plan and prepare a two-course meal well within £5 ($7) and still have some food – and change – left over. Rhian reports, 'This is a tried-and-tested regular meal: turkey spaghetti Bolognese with fresh tomatoes, and organic fruit yoghurt for dessert. I usually keep a portion of the Bolognese for my lunch

the next day so it serves five people, not four. I went to a well-known international supermarket chain to buy the ingredients.' The breakdown is:

 turkey mince £1.78 ($2.50)
 own-brand mushroom pasta sauce 88p ($1.20)
 own-brand basics range value spaghetti 39p (55c)
 organic plum tomatoes 66p (90c)
 biopot wholegrain peach yoghurt £1.24 ($1.70)

Total £4.95 ($6.90*)

(*North American readers should bear in mind that many prices in the States will be comparable to the UK, so mushroom sauce, for example, might be 88c a can, not the equivalent of 88p with the exchange rate applied.)

Stretching the Family Meal

There is a lot to be said for leftovers! In the preceding chapters we looked at a rough meal plan that showed how you can plan ahead when you shop so that you only buy what you really need for the week. And we have shown you how to look for and buy food at cheap prices while still making a varied meal. This section looks more in-depth at how to make a meal out of just a few ingredients, using leftovers in resourceful ways, avoiding wastage and making your own so you do not have to spend lots of money buying items such as sauces and stocks.

Making a Meal Go Further

If you are running low on ingredients, there is no need to rush for the nearest store to stock up. Take a look around at what you do have first, as this will save you time and money.

Thicken it Up!

If you are cooking a casserole or stew, but do not think there is enough meat or prime ingredient to go round, thicken it up with one or more of the following:

- peas
- lentils (red lentils cook more quickly than green lentils)
- rice
- can of sweetcorn
- chopped or diced potatoes
- pasta shapes

Short on Vegetables ...

If you do not have enough vegetables to accompany a meal, instead of buying new ones, think about making them up into a 'sauce' by adding a little stock and ketchup, or some chopped tomatoes, or some tomato soup.

... Long on Staples?

Do not just add more staple food to the plate to make it look like there is more food! Think about how to make it more interesting – it could be as simple as adding caraway seeds and black beans to rice, or mashing onion, mustard or leftover broccoli into mashed potatoes.

Make Salads Interesting

If you have only got a little bit of cucumber and tomato, but a lot of lettuce, think about adding some or all of the following to bulk it up:

- chopped pickled onions
- pickled beetroot slices
- grated carrot
- nuts or seeds
- chopped green grapes
- small dices of apple
- olives
- cold boiled egg

Be Bold

Be willing to try adding new or different ingredients, but please account for tastes:

- **Low on minced/ground beef?** Try bulking up your bolognese sauce with a little sausage or chopped ham.

- **Running low on cheese?** Make a herby white sauce to cover the cauliflower or macaroni, and then grate the small piece of cheese on top of the dish before cooking.

- **Thicken soups:** Add pureed potato (boil it up and blend it to a pulp) to soups and broths to thicken them.

- **Liven up yoghurt:** Use crushed cereal and honey to decorate yoghurt for a quick dessert.

- **Oaty crumble topping:** Mix oats and flour to create crumble toppings if you are low on flour.

- **Improve pizzas:** Jazz up plain pizzas with leftover pepper, tomatoes and sweetcorn.

Things to Avoid

We have all made disasters in our time, but really, do not try something weird, such as reheating yesterday's chips, putting fish into a meat dish to stretch it further or rustling up baked potato and chips. If you are not sure if your idea will work, try making a *little* bit in a separate bowl and tasting that first. Otherwise you will ruin all the ingredients and just throw your money away.

Learning from the Experts

They knew how to stretch food in the 1940s. With rationing came a restriction on everything from sugar to stockings, sweets to bananas. The rationing on sweets was not even lifted until the late 1950s, so they had to learn to make the most of what they had. They did not even have the option of going out and buying more – when food ran out in your house, it was probably running out in the shops too.

Creativity is Key

In *The Victory Cookbook*, Marguerite Patten OBE, who used to work for the UK's Ministry of Food during the Second World War, provided some brilliant recipes from cooks and caterers who learned to stretch the few ingredients they had:

- **Linda McCartney was not the first veggie sausage maker**: Factory canteen staff in the war years came up with lentil sausages (lentils, leeks, mashed potato and a little flour and seasoning).

- **Eggless sponge**: With farming stretched to full capacity, eggs were rationed and not every household could buy even powdered egg at times. There are a number of ingredients that can be used instead of eggs in baking recipes.

- **Sugar stretching**: Using honey, fruit syrup and condensed milk to sweeten things when sugar was running low.

- **Cod and tomato fishcakes**: These, according to Patten, had very little fish in them, but the tomato and herbs more than made up for it.

New Dishes from Leftovers

You can always find ways to use those 'little bits' left over for the whole family to enjoy, rather than have one person eating them up or, worse, throwing them away. Waste not, want not...

Here are some examples:

Bubble 'n' Squeak

A classic for brunch or a light dinner, it uses odds and ends of potato, vegetables and meat, all bound together with an egg and fried (you can use low-fat oil instead of the traditional lard!). All the ingredients, except for the egg, should have been cooked beforehand. Simply dice the cold meat and vegetables, allowing one egg per person. Beat the eggs and then stir them into the meat and vegetables. Fry over a moderate heat for 10–15 minutes, turning after 5 minutes.

Rissoles

Another wartime classic, rissoles are a brilliant way of using leftovers without making your family groan with boredom. These can be made using any leftover cooked meat or veg, and will stretch a small amount of food. Simply dice the meat or veg and set aside, then, in a pan, make a white sauce from any leftover gravy or stock (made up with 300 ml/^{1}/$_2$ pt/1^1/$_4$ cups milk), some seasoning and 1 heaped tablespoon flour. After it boils, add the meat, spread it on to a plate, cool it down and add breadcrumbs. Then, shape it how you like, let it set for a while, then fry it up.

Vegetable or Meat Timbales

Using leftover minced/ground meat, canned ham or corn, or roast vegetables, this is very similar to rissoles, only it is steamed instead of being fried. Blend the meat or vegetables together with 25 g/1 oz/^{1}/$_4$ cup breadcrumbs, 1 egg and some herbs; make up a white sauce (see below for instructions) and mix this into the ingredients, along with salt and pepper; pour the mixture into greased moulds and steam for 20–30 minutes; serve with a small helping of plain pasta, lightly tossed with oil and parsley.

Meat Paste

This was popular in the interwar period during the 1920s and 1930s, used on toast, or as a cheap pâté with cheese, crackers and quince. Simply take the remainder of any cooked meat, mince it finely, add some herbs and spices and push through a sieve; mix it together with 50 g/2 oz/¼ cup butter and put it into jars, pouring a little melted butter over the top to seal in the flavour.

Multiple Remixes

There are so many ways to make each of the dishes above, and there are many more dinners that can be made out of what is left over. The objective of the cooks of yesteryear who came up with the idea of turning one day's meal into another completely different one was to prevent boredom as much as to protect the food budget. Nobody wants to eat the same thing two days in a row; with careful planning and a little bit of panache, easy dishes can stretch the leftover food into a delicious meal the following day without stretching your bank account.

One Day's Dinner is the Next Day's Lunch

Well, not necessarily the next day – you have the option of storing and saving it for a day or so later, for when you feel like it. But however you want to mix it up for variety, the fact remains that if you use leftovers wisely, you will save a lot of money by not having to spend on expensive lunches. Even if you 'only' spend a few pounds or dollars on lunch each day, every day for five days, this works out at quite a significant potential saving in the working week. Multiply that by 52 and you could knock a staggering sum off your yearly food budget.

Bake and Freeze

By making a little more than you would eat one day, you can save the remaining food for another. For example, suppose you bake a lasagne for six people, accompanied with salad or vegetables, but you are a family of four. You might have enough for two whole adult portions left over which you could freeze together or separately. This could become two days' worth of lunch, or a light meal another evening.

The Cold Roast Sandwich

Everyone knows the famous turkey sandwich, made the day after Thanksgiving or Christmas, with the leftover turkey meat and stuffing. But why not apply this 'rule' to every roast meal that you have? Doing this means that you will not need to throw away the leftover cuts of meat if there were only a few remaining post-roast; nor will you have to store a small amount in the fridge or freezer. Most importantly, feeding the family at lunchtime with delicious cold meat or roast vegetable sandwiches will save money by:

 Avoiding lunchtime purchases: Family members will not have to buy sandwiches (or any other temptations) at lunchtime the next day.

 Spending less on home-made sandwiches: You will not have to keep buying expensive sandwich fillers, or have to use them up so quickly.

Sad Salad

If you have had a salad the night before and there is only a dribble left, do not throw it out. It could be used in a sandwich, to garnish a baked potato, or bolstered up with a little more lettuce and chopped tomato and made into a light lunch the next day. Remember, the more you save, the less you need to buy – and the less you need to buy, the healthier your budget will be.

Soups, Stocks, Stuffings and Sauces

It is shocking when we consider how much we pay for shop-bought meat or pasta sauces, canned soups, condiments, stuffing and stock. Yet all these things can be made really cheaply with the ingredients we already have – and are using without knowing it – when we cook. They are really easy as well, so why do we not do it more often instead of spending? Here are just a few ideas to help you make your own and cut out a significant portion of your household food budget.

Apple Sauce

Apples that are going a little, well, wrinkly, are no good to eat but they *are* good for sauces and cooking. Instead of throwing them out, wash, peel, chop and boil them up with a little sugar and water and you have ready-made chunky apple sauce that can be used in pies, crumbles, preserves and to accompany pork.

White Sauce

Rather than buying expensive packet mixes or jars of white sauces, make them yourself by stirring a little flour into a saucepan with some melted butter, whisk in some milk, little by little, until it has all blended but not boiled. Stir continually. This is a basic white sauce, to which you could add pepper, if liked. To make it béchamel sauce, add some grated nutmeg and a little cream, or to make it cheese sauce, add some grated cheese and some herbs. To save on milk, use milk diluted with vegetable water.

Cheat's Soup

If you have not got enough leftovers for a sufficient portion for another meal, or even for bubble and squeak or rissoles, make the leftovers into a soup with the addition of lentils to thicken it into a hearty broth. Serve with cheese on toast. See the soups section for some ideas.

Pasta Sauce

This is great for lasagnes and uses up lots of bits of vegetable. If you have a sausage or piece of ham left over from a previous meal, chop this into tiny pieces, together with half a grated carrot and half a grated celery stick. You do not need wine. Add half an onion, fry the sausage or ham in a little oil, then add the onion and the rest of the grated vegetables. When they are starting to brown, add 150 g/5 oz minced/ground beef (you can buy basic or no-frills for this) and, when this is browned, add a large tin of tomatoes and some dried herbs. You can simmer this on a low heat for 40 minutes or in a slow cooker.

Vegetarian Spaghetti Bolognese Sauce

Chop up an old half or whole onion and brown in a frying pan in a little light cooking oil, then add a large tin of chopped tomatoes and any tomatoes which are looking a little over-ripe, some dried herbs and any bits of bell pepper or other vegetables that you have left in your fridge. Simmer and season with (vegetarian) Worcestershire sauce, or similar, to taste.

Stuffing

An easy recipe for this is cranberry and orange stuffing. This uses rice, so is good for people with a gluten allergy or intolerance. You will need:

50 g/2 oz/¹⁄₄ cup caster/superfine sugar

 300 ml/¹⁄₂ pt/1¹⁄₄ cups water

 grated rind and juice of 1 orange

 225 g/8 oz/2 cups frozen cranberries or jar of old cranberry sauce

 350 g/12 oz/1³⁄₄ cups long-grain rice

 75 g/3 oz/¹⁄₃ cup butter or margarine

 1 large onion, finely chopped

 ¹⁄₂ clove garlic (or to taste), crushed

 2 tbsp parsley, chopped (fresh is best, but dried also works)

 1 tbsp thyme, chopped

salt and/or pepper

Thaw the cranberries, if using frozen. In a saucepan, stir the sugar and water on a low heat until the sugar has dissolved, then boil for 2 minutes. Add the orange juice, rind and cranberries or cranberry sauce and stir gently. Simmer for about 5 minutes, then set aside to cool. Cook the rice in a large pan of salted water. When tender, drain it and rinse it in cold water. Melt the butter in a saucepan and fry the onion and garlic in it on a low heat for a few minutes. Mix the rice, herbs and cranberry-and-orange sauce mix into the onion and melted butter and season it to taste with pepper and/or salt. When cool, shape it into balls in your hand and roast alongside the meat, or stuff it into the chicken or turkey.

Make Your Own Stock

Stock is the liquid obtained when bones, meat, fish or vegetables have been simmered in water to extract the flavour. It is the basis of most soups, sauces, stews and gravies. So, instead of spending on packaged stock cubes or (worse) jars of sauce or gravy, make your own in typical 1930s style: the water in which meat, rice or vegetables have been boiled may be substituted for stock, so, if the household is large, a stockpot should be kept in the fridge, into which should be put all suitable scraps such as vegetable peelings, tomato skins, meat trimmings and leftover scraps – avoid starchy food such as potatoes as this makes it cloudy. Boil it up, skim off any fat, strain and use. If you are keeping it for more than a day, boil it up each day.

Resourceful Salad Dressings

Many families buy salad dressing which only gets used once or twice, then left to go mouldy in the fridge drawer. This is a waste and will damage the budget. But it is possible to make your own while using up the odds and ends of other jars and bottles. You need: the last bit of Dijon mustard, the remnants of the vinegar bottle and a scoop of honey (or whatever is left in the old jar). Mix them all together with a little warm, boiled water and you have a honey and mustard salad dressing.

Mix and Match

As you get more used to making your own soups and stocks, you can always start to vary the ingredients according to your family's tastes. You might like to experiment with ketchup, Marmite or soy sauce, add crushed walnuts to stuffings or bulk up your soups with blended potatoes or peas. By collecting recipes and thinking about maximizing the ingredients that you do have, you can cut back on buying those expensive soups and sauces that you do not need.

Creative Snacking

Rather than buy costly snack items or popular sugary treats (which usually tend to go much more quickly than you had budgeted for), why not try to minimize the snacks that you buy, and maximize the ones you make using the leftovers? This is so cost-effective and they do not have to take a long time to make, either.

Why Make Your Own Snacks?

Making your own snacks has several advantages:

✓ **No hidden surprises:** You can watch exactly how much sugar, fat and salt goes into the home-made snacks. Equally, you can cater for family members with special dietary needs, without worrying about checking packets all the time.

✓ **Quantity:** You can make as much as you need, not more.

✓ **Efficient use of ingredients:** You can use up ingredients that are running low, rather than throw them out; or you will find there are many core ingredients left for another cooking session.

✓ **Family fun:** Cooking and baking with the family involved really can be a fun (and inexpensive) activity; it also teaches them valuable life-skills.

Snacks You Can Make

The following are ideas for snacks to make from what is left over – some of which would be much more expensive if you bought them in the shops. We will look at how to make some of these here; for other quick desserts, see the recipes on pages 240–253. While none of these is exactly healthy, they are a fun indulgence.

✓ **cheese straws**
✓ **cheese on toast**
✓ **ice cream soda floats**
✓ **bread-and-butter pudding**
✓ **fridge squares**
✓ **cereal cakes**

Cheese Straws

A little bit of cheese could be eaten by one person in one go, but why not mix together a little pastry dough, roll it out flat, score it into thin slices and grate the cheese over the top? After 20 minutes in the oven, you have lovely cheese straws that the whole family can share and it has hardly cost you anything.

Ice Cream Soda Floats

If you do not have enough ice cream to go round one evening, why not make ice cream floats instead of digging into a new tub? They are super quick. Simply add one scoop of ice cream to some cola or lemonade, stick a funky straw in and hey presto!

Fridge Squares

These are cobbled together with whatever is around: bits of broken biscuits, leftover raisins, nuts, chopped glacé cherries. The ingredients are bundled together with melted sugar, butter and chocolate, poured into a cake tin and cooled.

Cereal Cakes

If the cereal is nearing its use-by date, or it is not popular and likely to be wasted, you can do the following:

- **Nests:** Stir flakes or shredded wheat cereals into melted chocolate and pat into 'nest' shapes. You can fill these with jelly beans, chocolate mini-eggs or coated peanuts.

- **Cup cakes:** Mix cornflakes or rice cereals into melted chocolate, scoop into cupcake holders and chill.

- **Slabs:** Melt marshmallows, leftover Mars bars or a mixture of golden syrup, sugar and butter; mix with the cereal and place into a cake tray. Cool, then drizzle melted chocolate on top.

Maximize the Meal, Minimize the Spend

Hopefully, this has given you more of an idea about how to use up the leftovers, without resorting to throwing them out. It is not about using up the scraps left over on people's plates, but about what is left in the pots after serving up the right portions for each person and making the most of the little bits and bobs in your fridge and cupboards to maximize your meals and minimize your spend. For more ideas, check out www.lovefoodhatewaste.com.

Storing Food

It sounds like common sense, but storing food is not something that many families today find easy, for various reasons. We tend to throw away what is left if we think it is 'too small a portion' or we cannot think where to put it. Sometimes we need to think about ways of storing it that will get the best out of that particular food. Then there is the question of cupboard space... Here are a few helpful pointers to make your food stretch further and keep safer.

The Big Freeze

Forget stuffing frozen pizzas, pies and ready meals into your freezer. In reality, you can freeze just about anything for a future date. Often, fridge-freezers or deep-freezer units will display on their doors the ideal length of time for various food groups to help you work out for how long food can be stored.

What Can You Freeze?

What can't you freeze? Did you know you can freeze:

- milk
- fruit
- vegetables
- soups
- stews
- leftovers
- takeaways
- bread (bagels, buns and fruit loaf too)

Special Offers

Buying 'big ticket' items such as meat or fish fillets on a two-for-one or special offer is a great idea. Make the most of this and buy twice as much (because you will save more in the long term). These are often in freezable containers already so storing these is easy to do (make sure you have room!).

Bake 'n' Freeze

Many families cook extra portions and freeze them ready for another meal, another day. This may seem like extra work, but cooking up all your 'old' vegetables, for example, into a stew and freezing it reduces food wastage and saves money. And some days, you just cannot find the time to cook; being able to simply open the freezer and find your meal ready-made is a blessing.

Keeping Your Freezer Clean

This may sound obvious but, when your freezer is chock-full of ice and frost, it can create problems, such as:

- **A premium on space:** When the freezer is overly frosted, you cannot store as much as you would like to.

- **Inefficient use of energy:** Because it is frosted up, the freezer has to work twice as hard to keep things cold. Therefore, it is using more energy. Because it is using more energy, it is ratcheting up your fuel bills.

- **Blocked drainage:** Too much frost and ice can block up the freezer or fridge drainage, meaning leaks from the unit on to the floor.

- **The hassle of defrosting:** Defrosting a freezer can take a long time and, if you chip away at the ice with a knife, this can damage the knife, the freezer or even you.

Tips for Efficiency

To keep your freezer or icebox at maximum efficiency, bear in mind the following:

 Not too high: Keep it at a lower temperature setting – try turning it from 6 to 5, for example.

 Regular turnover: Check regularly to see what food has been in the freezer for too long, and use it up.

 A helping hand: Try using an anti-frost mat, which can be bought inexpensively over the internet or from most homeware stores.

Stocking Cupboards

There is a lot to be said for buying in bulk or getting family-sized packs of food, but not if you let something fester in the back of your cupboard or your kitchen larder. That said, there are many food items which can be stored for a much longer time than you think outside of the fridge or freezer. This might help when you bulk buy or wonder what you are going to cook.

Dried Food

We have explored the benefits of staple dried food such as pasta or rice, but here are a couple more pointers to help you live on a tight family budget without feeling the pain:

 Longevity of dried food: It is worth stocking up on dried split peas, lentils, rice and other dried foodstuffs. They can keep for up to 18 months or more, meaning they can always be relied on for a rainy day. If you have bought in bulk, dried foods can last for a long time without you having to replace them.

Clean and dry means less waste: When a bag of rice has split, or the pasta box is nearly empty, do not just leave it in the cupboard; put the rest into a jar or small tin, label it well and put into the cupboard. This will help to keep it fresher for longer and reduce any accidental spillage.

Canned Food Pros

This also has longevity, but we are not advocating constructing a mini-Warhol of soup cans in your kitchen. However, tinned food has several advantages:

 Longevity equals bulk: Since it has such a long shelf life, tinned food can be bought in bulk without fear of wastage or the need to freeze.

 Versatility: It can be used on its own, cold or as part of a cooked meal; soups can be used as sauces or thickeners for stews; and cans of beans, spaghetti hoops and similar items make quick, light and cheap meals.

 Low cost: Most shops sell good quality, low-cost versions of the big-name brands.

 Convenience: Canned food is handy for days when you are ill or cannot get out to buy fresh ingredients.

Canned Food Cons

Watch out for:

 Rust: Rusting on tins can be caused by steam and damp created by cooking, so cook with a window open or fan on where possible.

 Dents: In tins with dents that have 'pierced' through to the contents, the food is probably off.

Bulges: Tins which are bulging should be steered clear of – the food is definitely off.

Store-cupboard Essentials

Here is a list of some items you should probably always ensure that you have in your cupboard – it is not an exhaustive list, of course, as everyone has their own products that are indispensable to their store cupboard:

- dried herbs and spices
- tinned soup
- tinned beans
- tinned fish
- dried noodles
- dried pasta
- rice
- corned beef
- tinned tuna
- tea bags
- peanut butter
- long-life milk (handy for 'emergencies')
- chilli sauce
- cocoa powder (for cooking and drinking)
- custard powder
- basic mixes for jellies/jellos
- jams/jellies and marmalade (but see below for making your own)
- soy sauce
- ketchup
- cooking oil (good quality, virgin olive oil is worth it)
- a nice wine vinegar
- salsa or Tabasco sauce
- Worcestershire sauce

Store-cupboard Non-essentials

There are, however, many items that may be appropriate (or more realistic) for a student's store cupboard, but which are a false economy for a family's budget and health, or should be made rather than bought:

- **Tinned pulses and beans:** It is better to buy these dry and in bulk as they are cheaper and last longer – although it involves forethought as they may need long soaking.

- **Microwave rice:** This is OK, but it is far better to buy bulk and make up your own.

- **Pasta-bake sauces:** Not for the family – it is far cheaper to make your own.

- **Tinned fruit and veg:** This can be useful for trifles and pies, but steer clear of tinned vegetables except perhaps sweetcorn or butter beans.

- **Tinned meat pies:** Big no-no for the family – cook your own out of leftovers to save several bucks. Same goes for tinned meat curry.

- **Tinned red salmon:** Pink salmon is cheaper in tins, while mackerel and sardines are even cheaper.

Making the Most of 'Expensive' Items

Food such as dried herbs and spices, cooking oils and sauces are high-ticket items and can push the cost of your shopping trolley up significantly. But they are worth their weight in gold:

- they last a long time
- herbs, spices and sauces help to make meals more flavoursome
- you only need to use a little each time
- there are often deals on good-quality cooking oils

Thinking Laterally

Nice wine vinegars or 'posh' oils can make good presents and gifts.... Spices that fit into a spice rack are inexpensive 'gifts' that children can buy to help form a collection.

Out of Sight, But Not Out of Mind (Completely)

All these products we have discussed can be put away into the cupboard and forgotten about until they are needed. But do make sure you check use-by dates, as it is easy to forget just how long some store-cupboard staples have been loitering on your shelves.

Storing Fruit and Vegetables

Many fruit and vegetables can be kept fresh, dried out, made up into preserves or sauces or even frozen whole. This makes it more than worthwhile to stock up when you see a great bargain on fresh produce or to start growing your own fresh fruit and vegetables! Here we look at storing fruit around the house or in the fridge.

Stoned Fruit

This is not casting aspersions on their smoking habits. 'Stoned fruit' refers to fruit that has a central kernel, or stone. These tend to be softer fruit, which are more easily bruised, and may require different approaches to storing, compared with 'hard' fruit such as apples or pears. Although tomatoes do not have a stone, they are a soft fruit and can be stored in the same way as soft fruit can. Examples of stoned fruit are: apricots, avocados, cherries, lychees, nectarines, peaches and plums. Eat stoned fruit within a week, and bear the following in mind:

- **Choosing**: Select unwrinkled, smooth-skinned fruits with no blemishes, free of soft spots or discolouration. This will ensure maximum life and quality.

- **Storing ripe fruit**: Refrigerate ripe stoned fruit in a plastic bag and use within four days.

✔ **Ripening hard fruit**: If the fruit is a little hard, leave it at room temperature for a few days to soften up, but check to make sure it is not getting overripe.

✔ **Just before eating**: Any fruit whose skin you eat along with the flesh should be washed in running water to make sure you remove any harmful bacteria or dirt.

Hard Fruit

Hard fruit mainly describes apples, pears and pineapples. Different rules apply when storing each of these three fruit. It is not hard to store apples, as you can leave them for months on end before they go past the point of no return. This makes them an excellent budget food, as well as being versatile and able to be eaten fresh or cooked. The more ripe the apple, the longer it stores. Pears do not keep as long as apples – maybe a month or two maximum. Pineapples do not keep well at room temperature, and are best in the fridge. However, they can be frozen, juiced or pulped. Bear the following in mind if storing hard fruit outside of the fridge:

✔ **Ventilation**: Hard fruit needs plenty of ventilation, so do not pack too closely together, and store in containers which are not airtight, such as a wooden bin or fruit crate. You can also store the fruit in plastic bags, as long as there is a hole in it to allow the air to circulate.

✔ **Temperature**: If you can, keep the temperature between 3°C/37°F and 7°C/44°F. So, obviously, the main part of the house may not be the best place if you want the fruit to last a while – ideal places are attics, cellars, garden sheds or garages.

✔ **Light**: Hard fruit stores longer if kept in the dark, another reason for storing the fruit in the locations suggested above.

☑ **'Bad influence'**: Overripe or decaying fruit can have an adverse effect on surrounding fruit. Check the fruit for any 'bad' ones and throw them away.

☑ **Apples and pears**: Apples keep well when wrapped in paper such as old newspaper or wrapped in straw. This protects them against contamination from any 'bad apples' as well. Pears need even more gentle handling, but do not like to be wrapped up.

Berries

This includes raspberries, blueberries, gooseberries, redcurrants, strawberries (which are not technically berries), blackcurrants, elderberries and blackberries. They all tend to go off within a few days at room temperature, and within a week in the fridge. However, they do freeze well, apart from strawberries (which might be best made up into a jam or preserve). Kiwi fruit should also be treated in the same way.

Citrus Fruit

This term includes lemons, limes, clementines, satsumas, oranges, grapefruit, mandarins, tangerines, kumquats and ugli fruit.

☑ **A sliding scale**: The most perishable citrus fruit is the loose-skinned tangerine, which keeps up to a week in the fridge. Other oranges can be refrigerated for two weeks or more. Lemons and limes can store for even longer in the fridge.

☑ **Fridge is best**: Citrus fruit keeps better in the fridge than the fruit bowl.

☑ **Wrapped but ventilated**: Store them in a plastic bag, which has air ventilation, in the fridge.

Bananas

These are very difficult to store as, if you put them in a fruit bowl, they will ripen the other fruit and cause them to go off. The same thing will happen if you put it in the fridge with other fruit (and tomatoes). Also, banana skins will go black in the fridge, while, if you chop them up, they will oxidize and turn brown, as do apples. Some tips for storing bananas are:

- ☑ **Segregation:** Keep bananas away from other fruit by keeping them in a separate bowl or hanging them on a banana tree (which also protects them from bruising). Or keep them in a plastic bag for a few days at room temperature.

- ☑ **Protection:** Store individual bananas in a 'banana case' to protect them from bruising when in your bag, for example. Check out www.bananaguard.com or www.bananabunker.com.

- ☑ **Preservation:** Cover chopped bananas with a little lemon or orange juice before using them on pies or desserts.

- ☑ **Preparation:** Freeze them whole when ripe, in a plastic bag. When they are defrosted they are perfect for cooking as there is little need to blend them.

Storing Root Vegetables

Root vegetables (carrots, parsnips, turnips, swedes/rutabagas, potatoes), especially ones you have grown yourself, can be stored in a cool, covered place such as an attic, porch, garage, garden shed or cellar. They store well loosely laid out in wooden boxes or crates and, like apples, they like to be individually wrapped in paper or packed with straw, or you can layer them with newspaper and plenty of sand to keep them cool. Remove loose soil but do not wash the vegetables before storing, and clear out any rotten or bad vegetables.

Bulb Vegetables

Onions and garlic that you have grown yourself must be thoroughly dried out first, perhaps for two weeks in the sun, until the outer skins are dark and crackly, like paper. Trim the stems and store them in boxes or string bags, but keep them cool and in the shade.

Bins and Barrels

Some fruit and vegetables will keep for a long time in a cupboard or 'vegetable bin'. Onions, garlic, turnips and potatoes will keep well in a clean, dry wooden box in a cool cupboard and apples and hard pears (conference) will keep well in a clean, dry box or barrel.

Freezing Fruit and Vegetables

Freezing fruit is easy and can be done in many ways. Most fruits maintain a high level of quality for eight to 12 months at freezing temperatures. Citrus fruit and juices keep for less – up to 6 months. Food may still be edible after these times, but may not taste as good. You can freeze fruit either as it is or in syrup.

Freezing Fruit on Its Own

Unsweetened fruit will keep for a shorter amount of time than fruit with syrup. Here are some tips:

- **Preparation:** Wash and prepare the fruit whole, halved or in quarters. If cutting into halves and quarters, discard any stones or cores.

- **Cooking:** Apples, rhubarb, pears and plums freeze better if they are cooked first. Add a little brown sugar syrup to sharper apples and rhubarb, especially if they are cut up. This prevents oxidization.

- **Bags of berries:** Berries (except strawberries) should be frozen on a flat tray first for a few hours, then put into individual bags and labelled.

- **Whole fruit:** Pack whole fruit into containers, leaving 2.5 cm/^{1}/$_2$ in headspace as the fruit will expand when frozen. Seal, label and freeze.

Freezing Fruit in Syrup

The sugar in syrup will help preserve fruit even longer. Pack the cut fruit into containers as described above, then:

 cover with cold syrup solution (1 part sugar to 1 part water)
 add ½ teaspoon ascorbic acid per 1l/1³/₄ pts/1 qt syrup
leave 2.5 cm/¹/₂ in headspace
seal, label and freeze

Freezing Fruit for a Puree or Sauce

This is great for planning pie fillings or preserves. For fruit that is soft enough, press the raw fruit through a sieve (to remove pips) or blend it (if there are no pips). For firmer fruit, bring to the boil and then simmer it for 2 minutes in 250 ml/8 fl oz/1 cup water to every 1.8 kg/4 lb of fruit, then press through a sieve or blend. Mix in ¹/₂ tablespoon lemon juice and 200 g/7 oz/1 cup sugar (to taste, depending on tartness), to every 900 g/2 lb of puree. Pack into containers, leaving the same amount of headspace as before.

Freezing Juices

This is great for making into jams/jellies. When adding the sugar, use around 200 g/7 oz/1 cup to each 1l/1³/₄ pts/1 qt juice:

 press the fruit through a sieve
 simmer until soft in a saucepan with a shallow layer of water
 strain through a muslin or 'jam' cloth bag
 cool down the juice
 sweeten with sugar, to taste
 pour into a container, leaving room for expansion
 freeze

Vegetables

You can freeze most vegetables in the same way as for fruit, only without adding the sugar. This is great for making vegetable puree for baby food, for example, or for storing leftover vegetables to be made up into a sauce or stew at a later date. You can even make carrot or beetroot juice to add to special blends and create a healthy drink. For fresh, uncooked vegetables you may need to blanch them before freezing – check out www.gardenguides.com/how-to/tipstechniques/vegetables/freezing.asp for advice on freezing vegetables.

Tupperware Makes a Comeback

It is now common knowledge that HM the Queen of England likes to put her cereals in Tupperware tubs. Although there is a known phobia of plastic containers, called 'Tupperware anxiety', it is fair to say that the majority of households will benefit from investing in sets of Tupperware or similar plastic tubs and containers.

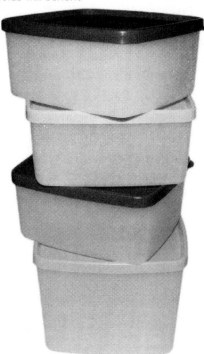

What Can You Put in Them?

You can put anything into them, including:

- soups
- stews
- fruit
- lasagne
- pasta dishes
- rice
- takeaways
- vegetables
- snacks
- salads
- curries

chocolate
 ice cream
 leftovers

Where Can You Put the Food Once It Is in the Tubs?

Anywhere! They can be put into the freezer, fridge or cupboard, depending on what you want to store. When you need it, you can put them into the microwave and they are also dishwasher friendly, although sometimes there can be slight discolouration depending on the type of dishwasher or detergent you use.

Other Benefits

Plastic containers are also useful for:

 Transporting food: Sandwiches, or a lunch you have prepared, can be taken to school, work or on a picnic.

 Protecting food: They can keep delicate food such as bananas safe from bruising.

 Using as a stockpot: You can keep a plastic tub in the fridge, into which you can put various materials appropriate for stock (see page 142).

 Keeping the air out: This way, cookies will not go soft and cakes will not go hard, for example.

 Keeping smells in: Well-sealed containers will prevent 'smell contagion' from strong cheeses or garlicky food, for example.

 Safety: Using well-sealed containers for different foodstuffs helps keep certain foods separate for family members with allergies, as well as raw meat separate from cooked meat or food.

Other Containers

This book is not about buying new tubs and pots to put your odds and ends of food in, but about helping you to save money. So look around at what you have in your house; you can make your budget go further if you use and reuse what you already have, rather than buying new.

Bags

If you do not have room in your icebox for pots and tubs, use heavy-duty, resealable freezer bags. Many of these can even be recycled, if you wash them out thoroughly and dry them before reusing.

Clips, Seals and Ties

Many freezer bags come with their own ties, but one often ends up using these for all sorts of food bags: open cereal packets, bags of potato chips or open bags of nuts, for example, all in an effort to keep food as fresh as possible without wastage.

- **Clips:** You can buy tough food bag clips to help keep dry food dry and prevent it from spilling out into the box or the cupboard. These can be washed and used again.

- **Clothes pegs:** Rather than buying special food ties or clips, you can use old wooden or plastic clothes pegs. Remember to wash and dry them first!

- **Old hair clips:** Children's discarded hair clips are great for using on dry food packets.

- **Elastic bands:** You may need different sizes depending on how big the packet is but rubber bands can be very versatile.

Sticky tape: This is great but is not reusable and often loses it stickiness before the packet is finished (the same goes for the resealable tabs that often come with packaging).

Reusing Containers

Rather than buy new tubs or pots, you can always make the most of the following:

 Takeaway containers: The plastic boxes from the Chinese takeout you had in a moment of weakness can be used in the same way as bought plastic boxes – in the fridge, freezer and microwave, and as lunchboxes.

 Ready-roast tins: If you buy frozen joints, they sometimes come in their own foil container. Shop-bought pies also have foil dishes that can be used to store or to cook in, if treated carefully – do not put foil in the microwave!

 Tins and cans: Keep those old coffee or biscuit tins: small cylindrical tins can be used to store the remnants of dried food such as rice or sugar; tall cylindrical tins can be used to store dried spaghetti; large round tins make excellent cake tins; and square tins can be used to store open flour or keep bread rolls fresh.

Labelling is Critical

Whether you are freezing or storing food for a shorter period of time, it is vital that you label things clearly, especially if you have put one foodstuff into another's container. As well as reminding you of the contents of a container, it also enables you to check the date you froze or stored the food in order to know whether it should still be edible or not. Even if *you* can remember what you have put in a certain container, clear labelling enables other members of the family to know what it is, what ingredients are in it and to identify food that may be unsuitable for those with special dietary needs. Clear labelling also facilitates quick identification when in a hurry.

Keeping Things out of Reach

One of the best ways to keep costs down often involves willpower! Snacking is fine every now and then, but often people tend to 'graze' on whatever they find around. If you have teenagers, you will know they have a predisposition towards eating everything that is in the house, despite having eaten three hearty meals during the day.

Lock the Cupboard

You may already lock the alcohol cupboard, but why not put more expensive snacks such as chocolates in a locked cupboard? Treats are not prohibited from the family's budget, but they can go very quickly so, by keeping hold of the key, they remain as treats, not as something to be munched throughout the day.

Out of Sight, Out of Reach

For smaller children, putting snacks and tasty treats into a particular tub and in a top cupboard may be a good way to stop little fingers getting to them. However, please make sure that your child does not get to know where they are – climbing accidents do happen frequently in the home. Try moving the snack box around to different locations every now and then.

Doing it by Halves

One pensioner tricks her twenty-something boys by taking half of her savoury snacks out of the box and hiding them in another container. This means they cannot eat *everything*.

Set Aside a Box for Special Dietary Needs

If you have diabetic-friendly snacks, or some gluten-free cakes, make sure the family knows that the box is only for the family member who has specific allergies or intolerances. Make sure it is labelled clearly.

Energy: The Hidden Cost of Cooking

During the research for this book, many people stated that they struggle not only with the price of food or even the cost of fuel in driving to the shop, but also the high cost of gas and electricity. Even with the price of crude oil falling by 50 per cent over 2008, from $80 per barrel of Brent crude to $40 by the end of the year, this still has some way to go to feed through to the price of fuel for your car, gas and electricity.

The Economy of Cooking

In 1936, the South Metropolitan Gas Company of the UK produced the *Metro Recipe Book* to help cash-strapped families recovering from the aftermath of the Great Depression. Its tips on how to save energy while cooking are as applicable today as they were more than 70 years ago:

Quality, Not Quantity

"True economy in the use of gas is not using a small quantity but getting the utmost value out of the gas consumed – making full use of the gas you are paying for." Keep to the cooking times recommended on the food item.

Double Up!

"It will be found an economy in time and gas if the cook plans meals days ahead. For example, if apples are being stewed, double quantity could be cooked to make a cold sweet for the following day. Or, cook a dish that could be served cold the next day and avoid waste space in the oven."

Think to Save Time

"Never light the gas without considering whether any other dishes might be cooked at the same time."

Keep it Clean!

"A clean cooker means an efficient one." The bars, burners, hotplate, oven door, grills and base of modern gas and electric ovens are all removable and can be cleaned easily. Tip: rub frying pans and grills/broilers over with newspaper while they are still hot, to save time washing up.

Use Residual Heat

"Residual heat is left in the oven after the oven has been turned off. Bread or crusts may be put in to dry to be made into dry breadcrumbs, for example." You could also use it to defrost something more quickly or warm the plates before serving a meal.

Position Food Properly

Cooking times can be reduced if you put food in the right place in the oven. Remember that lower shelves are cooler than top ones in a non-fan gas oven ('fan' or 'convection' gas ovens circulate the air, resulting in more even cooking). *Metro* suggests:

 Bread: Put a browning sheet at the top of the oven and place the bread below it. Reduce the heat once the bread has browned.

 Cakes: For small cakes, place them at the top of the oven under the browning sheet, on a moderately hot oven. For large cakes, remove the browning sheet and place the cake on a grid shelf in the centre of a moderate oven; reduce the heat as the cake bakes.

Joints: You do not need the browning sheet in the oven. Place the joint in the centre of the oven.

 Pastry: Put the browning sheet at the top of the oven and place the pastry close under it. Once it has browned, reduce the heat or put the pastry on a lower shelf to finish more slowly.

Slow Cookers

Relatively cheap to buy, and using only a low heat, you can use these electrical cookers to do a variety of delicious meals. They are safe, so can be left on while you are out at work, and only use a small amount of electricity. Here are some things you can cook:

 slow roasts (lamb, beef joints, chicken)
 casseroles
 stews
 moussaka
 **shepherd's or fisherman's pie**
 soups
 fish dishes
 pasta 'bakes'

The Gas Energy Saver

This is a relatively new invention that sits on top of the gas rings on your hob top and aims to cut down on the amount of wasted gas that is burned up inefficiently by most gas hobs. It has a catalytic, stainless alloy disc that notches safely on to the gas hob above the burner and converts all the unburnt gas to energy, heating to more than 100°C/212°F instantly. You can buy them over the internet or from most home and hardware stores. Since it enables a more efficient use of gas, it has several advantages:

reduces cooking time

 saves energy

 saves money – apparently up to 14 per cent off your gas bill

 cheap to buy (around £7/$10)

The Hay Box

You may be surprised at this eco-friendly way to cook your casseroles – and at how many people have installed one in their kitchens, garages or conservatories. The hay box is even internationally recognized; back in April 2008, *The New York Times* was advocating it as a way to reduce cooking bills and your family's carbon footprint. It is also a great way to save yourself time instead of slaving over a stove or waiting in while the dinner cooks.

What is It?

It is basically a wooden box or wicker basket, about the size of a small microwave, stuffed with hay, straw, banana leaves or barley husks. You can make it with offcuts of wood you find hanging around in your shed or garage and even use old newspaper (before you recycle it, of course). Kids will love to help make this – and love to use it for meals!

How Does it Work?

It is effectively a natural slow cooker. These materials are heat-retentive so they not only trap the heat of a partially cooked meal into it, but they keep the food hot, slow-cooking it over a period of hours. As an example, if you want to cook a really cheap cut of meat, such as beef skirt, which is tasty but notoriously tough, you can use this method:

 On the hob: Boil your tough cuts of meat, together with slow-cooking vegetables such as potatoes, on the stove for about 15 minutes maximum.

Season and embellish: Add ingredients such as herbs, spices and other vegetables (carrots, leeks, peas) while the meat is hot.

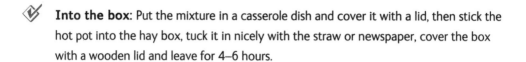

 Into the box: Put the mixture in a casserole dish and cover it with a lid, then stick the hot pot into the hay box, tuck it in nicely with the straw or newspaper, cover the box with a wooden lid and leave for 4–6 hours.

 Eat: When you return, the food has cooked all the way through and is tender, hot and tasty, without costing you anything in fuel bills *and* enabling you to go out without worrying about the place burning down.

Solar Cooking

If you live in a hot climate, try making your family dinners in a solar cooking box. This is very similar to the hay box, but uses light-trapping materials as solar panels, which then cook the food within the box. These can be made easily from odds and ends lying around your garage or shed.

Find Out More

For more information and instructions, visit these blogs and websites:

 www.howtopedia.org/en/How_to_Make_a_Cooking_Box_(Hay_Box_/_Hay_bag)

 www.cookinginabasket.blogspot.com

 www.hedon.info/goto.php/FirelessCooker

 www.solarcooking.org

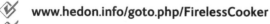

The Special Occasion

When it comes to special occasions, such as Christmas, birthdays, celebrations and other holidays, there is no need to skimp on the food budget and have a dreary time – if anything, we need to enjoy these times as much as possible as they are how we cheer ourselves up! As you will have realized by now – the key point of this book is to show that it is not about 'budgeting', really – it is about planning; and for special occasions, planning will come into its own.

Planning

Organizational skills are not genetic, they are as simple as making a list and thinking ahead – something everyone can do. We already spend time organizing things in our minds – the party, the guest list, the presents and who we are not going to send a card to again this year. So why not add food to this?

Saving for the Day

If you know there is a special occasion coming up, such as someone's 40th birthday, start saving up a little each month to cater for the extra expenditure on food and drink. Even a tenner a month for a year will give you a substantial extra sum to add to the shopping budget for that event. You never know, you might even get a smattering of interest accrued on it, even in this credit crunch.

Bulk Buying and Bargain Hunting

This is another occasion when bulk buying and bargain hunting can really make a significant difference to the food bill:

- **Search out special deals**: Two-for-one party foods or frozen finger-food are great buys – look out for these in the run-up.

- **Big can be better**: Giant packets of peanuts or candies bought from a bulk barn store will be cheaper per kg/lb than lots of smaller packets from a superstore.

- **Redeeming coupons and vouchers**: Keep your coupons for such a time as this! If you can, redeem them against expensive items such as alcohol.

- **Loyalty cards**: Trade in those loyalty points – you have earned them (also, if you use them up during the year at these times, if you ever lose the card, someone else will not benefit from loads of points).

Make Your Own

For even better savings, why not take some time to bake it up yourself? Many great party dishes can be made using leftovers and small portions of various ingredients. Even if you have to buy some of the ingredients for the purpose, many of these, such as flour or sugar, can be dipped into many times and stored away before they are used up. Plus, if you can bake four good-sized cakes (serving 8–10) for the price of a few ingredients, you should weigh this up against the cost of buying four cakes that serve the same number of people.

Using Up the Leftovers

In an earlier chapter, we looked at various snack items that could be baked together with younger family members, such as soda floats. But there are many other party dishes that can be made cheaply using bits and bobs you have lying around:

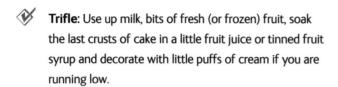

Trifle: Use up milk, bits of fresh (or frozen) fruit, soak the last crusts of cake in a little fruit juice or tinned fruit syrup and decorate with little puffs of cream if you are running low.

Fruit punch (alcoholic or non-alcoholic): Just use what you have left, tasting as you go (but no double-dipping of the spoon!).

Banoffee pie: Crushed or broken biscuits, sliced bananas, toffee or caramel sauce and small dollops of cream can be combined for a cheat's version of banoffee pie.

Clever canapés: Chopped tomatoes, grated cheese and herbs on any remaining bread can be cut up into hot little toasties; mini sausages can be partially sliced, filled with a tiny bit of mashed potato and turned into a baby bangers 'n' mash; a couple of small potato wedges and a small piece of breaded fish can be put into a wee paper cone for a take on fish and chips.

Fruit sticks: Fruit pieces can be skewered into small kebabs.

Party Like It's 1940!

Those clever folk living on rations knew how to throw a good street party, regardless of rationing and bombs. Even in the US and Canada, who had relatively uninterrupted lines of food transportation, most families were suffering and had to make do with what they had. They certainly came up with some delicious treats to tempt the blues away:

Cinnamon toast fingers: This was a Canadian favourite, mixing cinnamon with a little honey on buttered toast.

✅ **Baby doughnuts**: Made using small amounts of flour and sugar.

✅ **Glacé icing**: This used just water and icing/confectioners' sugar rather than Royal icing, which uses egg white.

✅ **Toffee apple slices**: These were slices lightly dipped in a sugar syrup, then cooled – a great American Sunday School picnic treat.

✅ **Fruit fritters**: These consisted of apples, plums, berries or pears fried up in a little sweet batter.

Baking v. Buying

As we have mentioned, when you buy cake from a shop, apart from the fact that it often tastes a little bit of cardboard and bitter preservatives, you can expect to pay a lot of money for one that will serve 8–10 people. True, if you buy the individual ingredients, these may add up to more than the cost of one shop-bought cake, but you have to look beyond the short term.

The Proof is in the Pudding

Suppose a large, shop-bought luxury chocolate cake with lovely icing, serving 8–10 people comes to just £10/$10. If you buy the individual ingredients yourself, to make a traditional Canadian family chocolate cake, you would need:

✅ **self-raising flour, or plain/all-purpose flour with 1 tsp baking powder**
✅ **butter, margarine or low-fat spread**
✅ **a 200 g/7 oz dark chocolate bar**
✅ **a 100 ml/3½ fl oz pot double/heavy cream**
✅ **150 g/5 oz/¾ cup caster/superfine or demerara/brown sugar**
✅ **eggs (packs of 12 work out cheaper per egg than a 6-pack)**
✅ **1 tin cocoa powder (suitable for drinking)**

What is Cheaper?

Initially, the cheaper product is the cake that is already in the box. But you have to think about what is left over...

What is Left Over?

True, half the chocolate bar has been melted into the butter and sugar and made up into cake mix. Some of the cream has gone into the cake mix, while the rest of the melted chocolate bar has been whisked into the double cream to make up a fluffy icing. But, you will have a ceratin number of ingredients left over:

- **Flour:** If you use 150 g/5 oz of a 1-kg/2¼-lb pack of flour, you will have 750 g/1⅔ lb left – enough for four more cakes and some white sauce mixture.

- **Butter:** If you use 125 g/4 oz of butter (roughly a ¼ pack), you still have enough left for three more cakes – or your daily usage.

- **Sugar:** If you use 150 g/5 oz of a 500 g/1 lb bag of sugar, you have 350 g/12 oz left – roughly ⅔ of the bag – enough for two more cakes or for other use.

- **Eggs:** You will have 10 eggs left – enough for five more cakes or for use in any family meal, breakfast, lunch or dinner.

- **Cocoa powder:** There is a lot of this left – and it lasts for months.

The proof really is in the pudding...

Recipes: Soups & Starters

PACKED WITH
• MONEY
SAVING •
IDEAS & TIPS •

Carrot and Ginger Soup

Ingredients (Serves 4)

4 slices bread, crusts removed
1 tsp yeast extract
2 tsp olive oil
1 onion, peeled and chopped
1 garlic clove, peeled and crushed
½ tsp ground ginger
450 g/1 lb carrots, peeled and chopped
1 l/1¼ pts/4 cups vegetable stock
2.5 cm/1 in piece root ginger, peeled and finely grated
salt and freshly ground black pepper
1 tbsp lemon juice

TO GARNISH:
chives
lemon zest

Preheat the oven to 180°C/350°F/Gas Mark 4. Roughly chop the bread. Dissolve the yeast extract in 2 table-spoons warm water and mix with bread.

Spread the bread cubes over a lightly oiled baking tray and bake for 20 minutes, turning halfway through. Remove from the oven and reserve.

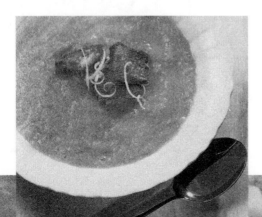

Heat the oil in a large saucepan. Gently cook the onion and garlic for 3–4 minutes.

Stir in the ground ginger and cook for 1 minute to release the flavour.

Add the chopped carrots, then stir in the stock and the fresh ginger. Simmer gently for 15 minutes.

Remove from the heat and allow to cool a little. Blend until smooth, then season to taste with salt and pepper. Stir in the lemon juice. Garnish with the chives and lemon zest and serve immediately.

Tasty Tip

This soup would be delicious for special occasions, if served with a spoonful of lightly whipped cream, crème fraîche or sour cream. Serve with slices of bruschetta, which can easily be made by lightly grilling/broiling thick slices of ciabatta bread on both sides. While still warm, rub the top of the bruschetta with a whole, peeled clove of garlic and drizzle with a little good quality extra virgin olive oil.

Rice and Tomato Soup

Ingredients (Serves 4)

150 g/5 oz/¾ cup easy-cook basmati rice
400 g can/1¾ cups chopped tomatoes
2 garlic cloves, peeled and crushed
grated zest of ½ lime
2 tbsp extra virgin olive oil
1 tsp sugar
salt and freshly ground black pepper
300 ml/½ pt/1¼ cups vegetable stock or water

FOR THE CROUTONS:
2 tbsp prepared pesto sauce
2 tbsp olive oil
6 thin slices ciabatta bread, cut into 1 cm/½ in cubes

 Preheat the oven to 220°C/425°F/Gas Mark 7. Rinse and drain the basmati rice. Place the canned tomatoes with their juice in a large, heavy-based saucepan with the garlic, lime zest, oil and sugar. Season to taste with salt and pepper. Bring to the boil, then reduce the heat, cover and simmer for 10 minutes.

Add the boiling vegetable stock or water and the rice, then cook, uncovered, for a further 15–20 minutes, or until the rice is tender. If the soup is too thick, add a little more water. Reserve and keep warm, until the croutons are ready.

Meanwhile, to make the croutons, mix the pesto and olive oil in a large bowl. Add the bread cubes and toss until they are coated completely with the mixture. Spread on a baking sheet and bake in the preheated oven for 10–15 minutes, until golden and crisp, turning them over halfway through cooking. Serve the soup immediately, sprinkled with the warm croutons.

Budget Tip

This is such a budget-friendly soup as it uses those faithful staples of rice and canned tomatoes. And if you cannot get hold of ciabatta bread, do not worry – just use what you have.

Cream of Spinach Soup

Ingredients (Serves 6-8)

1 large onion, peeled and chopped
5 large plump garlic cloves, peeled and chopped
2 medium potatoes, peeled and chopped
750 ml/1¼ pts/3¼ cups cold water
1 tsp salt
450 g/1 lb spinach, washed and large stems removed
50 g/2 oz/¼ cup butter
3 tbsp flour
750 ml/1¼ pts/3¼ cups milk
½ tsp freshly grated nutmeg
freshly ground black pepper
6–8 tbsp crème fraîche or sour cream
warm foccacia bread, to serve

Place the onion, garlic and potatoes in a large saucepan and cover with the cold water. Add half the salt and bring to the boil. Cover and simmer for 15–20 minutes, or until the potatoes are tender. Remove from the heat and add the spinach. Cover and set aside for 10 minutes.

Slowly melt the butter in another saucepan, add the flour and cook over a low heat for about 2 minutes.

Remove the saucepan from the heat and add the milk, a little at a time, stirring continuously. Return to the heat and cook, stirring continuously, for 5–8 minutes, or until the sauce is smooth and slightly thickened. Add the freshly grated nutmeg or pepper to taste.

Blend the cooled potato and spinach mixture in a food processor or blender to a smooth puree, then return to the saucepan and gradually stir in the white sauce.

Season to taste with salt and pepper and gently reheat, taking care not to allow the soup to boil. Ladle into soup bowls and top with spoonfuls of crème fraîche or sour cream. Serve immediately with warm foccacia bread.

Helpful Hint

When choosing spinach, always look for fresh, crisp, dark green leaves. Use within 1–2 days of buying and store in a cool place until needed. To prepare, wash in several changes of water to remove any dirt or grit and shake off as much excess water as possible, or use a salad spinner. Remove the central stems only if they are large and tough – this is not necessary if you buy baby spinach leaves.

White Bean Soup with Parmesan Croutons

Ingredients (Serves 4)

3 thick slices white bread, cut into 1 cm/½ in cubes
3 tbsp groundnut/peanut oil
2 tbsp Parmesan cheese, finely grated
1 tbsp light olive oil
1 large onion, peeled and finely chopped
50 g/2 oz/½ cup unsmoked bacon lardons (or thick
  slices of bacon, diced)
1 tbsp fresh thyme leaves
2 x 400 g/2 14 oz cans cannellini beans, drained
900 ml/1½ pts/1 qt chicken stock
salt and freshly ground black pepper
1 tbsp prepared pesto sauce
50 g/2 oz piece/½ cup pepperoni sausage, diced
1 tbsp fresh lemon juice
1 tbsp fresh basil, roughly shredded

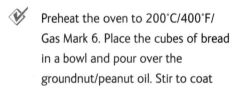 Preheat the oven to 200°C/400°F/ Gas Mark 6. Place the cubes of bread in a bowl and pour over the groundnut/peanut oil. Stir to coat

the bread, then sprinkle over the Parmesan cheese. Place on a lightly oiled baking tray and bake in the preheated oven for 10 minutes, or until crisp and golden.

Heat the olive oil in a large saucepan and cook the onion for 4–5 minutes until softened. Add the bacon and thyme and cook for a further 3 minutes. Stir in the beans, stock and black pepper and simmer gently for 5 minutes.

Place half the bean mixture and liquid into a food processor and blend until smooth.

Return the puree to the saucepan. Stir in the pesto sauce, pepperoni sausage and lemon juice and season to taste with salt and pepper.

Return the soup to the heat and cook for a further 2–3 minutes, or until piping hot. Place some of the beans in each serving bowl and add a ladleful of soup. Garnish with shredded basil and serve immediately with the croutons scattered over the top.

Creamy Chicken and Tofu Soup

Ingredients (Serves 4-6)

225 g/8 oz/½ lb firm tofu, drained
3 tbsp groundnut/peanut oil
1 garlic clove, peeled and crushed
2.5 cm/1 in piece fresh root ginger, peeled
 and finely chopped
2.5 cm/1 in piece fresh galangal, peeled
 and finely sliced (if available)
1 lemon grass stalk, bruised
¼ tsp ground turmeric
600 ml/1 pt/2½ cups chicken stock
600 ml/1 pt/2½ cups coconut milk
225 g/8 oz/2 cups cauliflower, cut into tiny florets
1 medium carrot, peeled and cut into thin matchsticks
125 g/4 oz/¾ cup green beans, trimmed
 and cut in half
75 g/3 oz thin egg noodles
225 g/8 oz/1 cup cooked chicken, shredded
salt and freshly ground black pepper

 Cut the tofu into 1 cm/½ in cubes, then pat dry on absorbent kitchen paper.

 Heat 1 tablespoon of the oil in a nonstick frying pan. Fry the tofu in 2 batches for 3–4 minutes or until golden brown. Remove, drain on absorbent kitchen paper and reserve.

 Heat the remaining oil in a large saucepan. Add the garlic, ginger, galangal and lemon grass and cook for about 30 seconds. Stir in the turmeric, then pour in the stock and coconut milk and bring to the boil. Reduce the heat to a gentle simmer, add the cauliflower and carrots and simmer for 10 minutes. Add the green beans and simmer for a further 5 minutes.

 Meanwhile, bring a large saucepan of lightly salted water to the boil. Add the noodles, turn off the heat, cover and leave to cook, or cook according to the packet instructions.

Remove the lemon grass from the soup. Drain the noodles and stir into the soup with the chicken and browned tofu. Season to taste with salt and pepper, then simmer gently for 2–3 minutes or until heated through. Serve immediately in warmed soup bowls.

Budget Tip
This is a great way of using chicken left over from that Sunday roast.

Sweetcorn and Crab Soup

Ingredients (Serves 4)

450 g/1 lb fresh corn on the cob
1.3 l/2¼ pts/5½ cups chicken stock
2–3 spring onions/scallions, trimmed
  and finely chopped
1 cm/½ in piece fresh root ginger, peeled
  and finely chopped
1 tbsp dry sherry or Chinese rice wine
2–3 tsp soy sauce
1 tsp light brown sugar
salt and freshly ground black pepper
2 tsp cornflour/cornstarch
225 g/½ lb white crabmeat, fresh or canned
1 medium/large egg white
1 tsp sesame oil
1–2 tbsp freshly chopped coriander/cilantro

Wash and dry the corn cobs. Using a sharp knife and holding the corn cobs at an angle to the chopping board, cut down along the cobs to remove the kernels, then scrape the cobs to remove any excess milky residue. Put the kernels and the milky residue into a large wok.

Add the chicken stock to the wok and place over a high heat. Bring to the boil, stirring and pressing some of the kernels against the side of the wok to squeeze out the starch to help thicken the soup. Simmer for 15 minutes, stirring occasionally.

Add the spring onions, ginger, sherry or Chinese rice wine, soy sauce and brown sugar to the wok and season to taste with salt and pepper. Simmer for a further 5 minutes, stirring occasionally.

Blend the cornflour with 1 tablespoon cold water to form a smooth paste and whisk into the soup. Return to the boil, then simmer over a medium heat until thickened.

Add the crabmeat, stirring until blended. Beat the egg white with the sesame oil and stir into the soup in a slow, steady stream, stirring constantly. Stir in the chopped coriander and serve immediately.

Oriental Minced Chicken on Rocket and Tomato

Ingredients (Serves 4)

2 shallots, peeled
1 garlic clove, peeled
1 carrot, peeled
50 g/2 oz/½ cup water chestnuts
1 tsp groundnut/peanut oil
350 g/12 oz fresh minced/ground chicken
1 tsp Chinese five-spice powder
pinch chilli powder
1 tsp soy sauce
1 tbsp fish sauce
8 cherry tomatoes
50 g/2 oz/1¼ cups rocket/arugula

 Finely chop the shallots and garlic. Cut the carrot into matchsticks, thinly slice the water chestnuts and reserve. Heat the oil in a wok or large, heavy-based frying pan and add the chicken. Stir-fry for 3–4 minutes over a moderately high heat, breaking up any large pieces of chicken.

 Add the garlic and shallots and cook for 2–3 minutes until softened. Sprinkle over the Chinese five-spice powder and the chilli powder and continue to cook for about 1 minute.

 Add the carrot, water chestnuts, soy and fish sauces and 2 tablespoons

water. Stir-fry for a further 2 minutes. Remove from the heat and reserve to cool slightly.

 Deseed the tomatoes and cut into thin wedges. Toss with the rocket and divide between four serving plates. Spoon the warm chicken mixture over the rocket and tomato wedges and serve immediately to prevent the salad from wilting.

Tasty Tip

This is a very versatile dish. In place of the chicken, you could use any lean cut of meat or even prawns/shrimp. To make this dish a main meal, replace the rocket and tomatoes with stir-fried vegetables and rice. Another alternative that works very well is to serve the chicken mixture in step 3 in lettuce leaves. Place a spoonful of the mixture into a lettuce leaf and roll up into a small parcel.

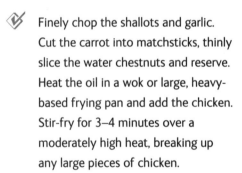

Swedish Cocktail Meatballs

Ingredients (Serves 4-6)

50 g/2 oz/½ stick butter
1 onion, peeled and finely chopped
50 g/2 oz/1 cup fresh white breadcrumbs
1 medium/large egg, beaten
125 ml/4 fl oz/½ cup double/heavy cream
salt and freshly ground black pepper
350 g/12 oz/1½ cups fresh lean minced/ground beef
125 g/4 oz/½ cup fresh minced/ground pork
3–4 tbsp freshly chopped dill
½ tsp ground allspice
1 tbsp vegetable oil
125 ml/4 fl oz/½ cup beef stock
cream cheese and chive or cranberry sauce, to serve

Heat half the butter in a large wok, add the onion and cook, stirring frequently, for 4–6 minutes, or until softened and beginning to colour. Transfer to a bowl and leave to cool. Wipe out the wok with kitchen paper.

Add the breadcrumbs and beaten egg with 1–2 tablespoons cream to the softened onion. Season to taste with salt and pepper and stir until well blended. Using your fingertips, crumble the beef and pork into the bowl. Add half the dill, the allspice and, using your hands, mix together until well blended. With dampened hands, shape the mixture into 2.5 cm/1 in balls.

Melt the remaining butter in the wok and add the vegetable oil, swirling it to coat the side of the wok. Working in batches, add about one quarter to one third of the meatballs in a single layer and cook for 5 minutes, swirling and turning until golden and cooked. Transfer to a plate and continue with the remaining meatballs, transferring them to the plate as they are cooked.

Pour off the fat in the wok. Add the beef stock and bring to the boil, then boil until reduced by half, stirring and scraping up any browned bits from the bottom. Add the remaining cream and continue to simmer until slightly thickened and reduced. Stir in the remaining dill and season if necessary. Add the meatballs and simmer for 2–3 minutes, or until heated right through. Serve with cocktail sticks, with the sauce in a separate bowl for dipping.

Potato Skins

Ingredients (Serves 4)

4 large baking potatoes
2 tbsp olive oil
2 tsp paprika
125 g/4 oz/³/₄ cup pancetta or bacon,
    roughly chopped
6 tbsp double/heavy cream
125 g/4 oz/¹/₃ cup Gorgonzola cheese
1 tbsp freshly chopped parsley

TO SERVE:
reduced-calorie mayonnaise
sweet chilli dipping sauce
tossed green salad

Preheat the oven to 200°C/400°F/Gas Mark 6. Scrub the potatoes, then prick a few times with a fork or skewer and place directly on the top shelf of the oven. Bake in the preheated oven for at least 1 hour, or until tender. The potatoes are cooked when they yield gently to the pressure of your hand.

Set the potatoes aside until cool enough to handle, then cut in half and scoop the flesh into a bowl and reserve. Preheat the grill/broiler and line the rack with kitchen foil.

Mix together the oil and the paprika and use half to brush the outsides of the potato skins. Place on the grill rack under the preheated hot grill and cook for 5 minutes, or until crisp, turning as necessary.

Heat the remaining paprika-flavoured oil and gently fry the pancetta until crisp. Add to the potato flesh along with the cream, Gorgonzola cheese and parsley. Fill the potato skins with the Gorgonzola filling. Return to the oven for a further 15 minutes to heat through. Sprinkle with a little more paprika and serve immediately with mayonnaise, sweet chilli sauce and a green salad.

Food Fact

A popular, well-known Italian cheese, Gorgonzola was first made over 1,100 years ago in the village of the same name near Milan.

Thai Crab Cakes

Ingredients (Serves 4)

225 g/8 oz/1 cup white and brown crabmeat (about
   equivalent to the flesh of 2 medium crabs)
1 tsp ground coriander
1/4 tsp chilli powder
1/4 tsp ground turmeric
2 tsp lime juice
1 tsp soft light brown sugar
2.5 cm/1 in piece fresh root ginger, peeled and grated
3 tbsp freshly chopped coriander/cilantro
2 tsp finely chopped lemon grass
2 tbsp plain/all-purpose flour
2 medium/large eggs, separated
50 g/2 oz/1 cup fresh white breadcrumbs
3 tbsp groundnut/peanut oil
lime wedges, to garnish
mixed salad leaves, to serve

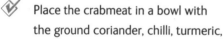 Place the crabmeat in a bowl with the ground coriander, chilli, turmeric, lime juice, sugar, ginger, chopped coriander, lemon grass, flour and egg yolks. Mix together well.

Divide the mixture into 12 equal portions and form each into a small patty about 5 cm/2 in across. Lightly whisk the egg whites and put into a dish. Place the breadcrumbs on a separate plate.

Dip each crab cake, first in the egg whites, then in the breadcrumbs, turning to coat both sides. Place on a plate, cover and chill in the refrigerator until ready to cook.

Heat the oil in a large frying pan. Add 6 crab cakes and cook for 3 minutes on each side, or until crisp and golden brown on the outside and cooked through. Remove, drain on absorbent kitchen paper and keep warm while cooking the remaining cakes. Arrange on plates, garnish with lime wedges and serve immediately with salad leaves.

Helpful Hint

If you buy fresh crabs, prepare them in the following way. Twist off the legs and claws, then crack them open and remove the meat. Turn the crab on to its back and twist off the bony, pointed flap. Place the tip of a knife between the main shell and where the legs were attached, twist the blade to lift up and remove, then scrape out the brown meat. Pull away and discard the soft, grey gills. Split the body in half and, using a skewer, remove the white meat from the cavities.

Prawn Toasts

Ingredients (Serves 8-10)

225 g/8 oz/2 cups cooked peeled prawns/shrimp,
   thawed if frozen, well drained and dried
1 medium/large egg white
2 spring onions/scallions, trimmed and chopped
1 cm/¹/₂ in piece fresh root ginger, peeled
   and chopped
1 garlic clove, peeled and chopped
1 tsp cornflour/cornstarch
2–3 dashes hot pepper sauce
¹/₂ tsp sugar
salt and freshly ground black pepper
8 slices firm-textured white bread
4–5 tbsp sesame seeds
300 ml/¹/₂ pt/1 ¹/₄ cup vegetable oil for deep frying
sprigs of fresh coriander/cilantro, to garnish

Put the prawns, egg white, spring
onions, ginger, garlic, cornflour, hot
pepper sauce and sugar into a food
processor. Season to taste with about
¹/₂ teaspoon of salt and black pepper.

Process until the mixture forms a
smooth paste, scraping down the side
of the bowl once or twice.

Using a metal palette knife, spread
an even layer of the paste evenly
over the bread slices. Sprinkle each
slice generously with sesame seeds,
pressing gently to bury them in
the paste.

Trim the crusts off each slice, then cut
each slice diagonally into 4 triangles.
Cut each triangle in half again to make
8 pieces from each slice.

Heat the vegetable oil in a large wok
to 190°C/375°F, or until a small cube
of bread browns in about 30 seconds.
Working in batches, fry the prawn
triangles for 30–60 seconds, or until
they are golden, turning once.

Remove with a slotted spoon and drain
on absorbent kitchen paper. Keep the
toasts warm. Arrange them on a large
serving plate and garnish with sprigs of
fresh coriander. Serve immediately.

Tasty Tip
This is a classic Chinese appetizer. Serve
it with a selection of other snacks as a
starter, or with drinks.

Recipes:
Fish &
Seafood

PACKED WITH • MONEY SAVING • IDEAS & TIPS •

Gingered Cod Steaks

Ingredients (Serves 4)

2.5 cm/1 in piece fresh root
    ginger, peeled
4 spring onions/scallions
2 tsp freshly chopped parsley
1 tbsp soft brown sugar
4 x 175 g/6 oz thick cod steaks
salt and freshly ground black pepper
25 g/1 oz/¼ stick butter or low-fat spread
freshly cooked vegetables, to serve

Preheat the grill/broiler and line the grill rack with a layer of kitchen foil. Coarsely grate the piece of ginger. Trim the spring onions and cut into thin strips.

Mix the spring onions, ginger, chopped parsley and sugar. Add 1 tablespoon water.

Wipe the fish steaks. Season to taste with salt and pepper. Place on to 4 separate 20.5 x 20.5 cm/8 x 8 in kitchen foil squares.

Carefully spoon the spring onion and ginger mixture over the fish.

Cut the butter into small cubes and place over the fish.

Loosely fold the foil over the steaks to enclose the fish and to make a parcel.

Place under the preheated grill and cook for 10–12 minutes, or until cooked and the flesh has turned opaque.

Place the fish parcels on individual serving plates. Serve immediately with the freshly cooked vegetables.

Helpful Hint

This recipe will also work well with other fish steaks. Try salmon, fresh haddock or monkfish fillets. The monkfish fillets may take a little longer to cook.

Chunky Halibut Casserole

Ingredients (Serves 6)

50 g/2 oz/¹/₄ cup butter or margarine
2 large onions, peeled and sliced into rings
1 red pepper/bell pepper, deseeded and
    roughly chopped
450 g/1 lb potatoes, peeled
450 g/1 lb courgettes/zucchini, trimmed and
    thickly sliced
2 tbsp plain/all-purpose flour
1 tbsp paprika
2 tsp vegetable oil
300 ml/¹/₂ pt/1¹/₄ cups white wine
150 ml/¹/₄ pt/²/₃ cup fish stock
400 g/14 oz can chopped tomatoes
2 tbsp freshly chopped basil
salt and freshly ground black pepper
450 g/1 lb halibut/white fish fillet, skinned and
    cut into 2.5 cm/1 in cubes
sprigs of fresh basil, to garnish
freshly cooked rice, to serve

Melt the butter or margarine in a large saucepan, add the onions and pepper and cook for 5 minutes, or until softened.

Cut the peeled potatoes into 2.5 cm/1 in dice, rinse lightly and shake dry, then add them to the onions and pepper in the saucepan. Add the courgettes and cook, stirring frequently, for a further 2–3 minutes.

Sprinkle flour, paprika and vegetable oil into the saucepan and cook, stirring continuously, for 1 minute. Pour in 150 ml/¹/₄ pt/²/₃ cup of the wine, with all the stock and the chopped tomatoes, and bring to the boil.

Add the basil to the casserole, season to taste with salt and pepper and cover. Simmer for 15 minutes, then add the halibut and the remaining wine and simmer very gently for a further 5–7 minutes, or until the fish and vegetables are just tender. Garnish with basil sprigs and serve immediately with freshly cooked rice.

Food Fact

Halibut is a flatfish with firm, milky white flesh that has an almost meaty texture, making it ideal for this casserole. They can grow to an enormous size, at times weighing in at over 200 kg/ 444 lb, and are fished in the deep, freezing cold waters of the North Sea.

Fish Crumble

Ingredients (Serves 6)

450 g/1 lb whiting or halibut fillets
300 ml/½ pt/1¼ cups milk
salt and freshly ground black pepper
1 tbsp sunflower oil
75 g/3 oz/⅓ cup butter or margarine
1 medium onion, peeled
    and finely chopped
2 leeks, trimmed and sliced
1 medium carrot, peeled and
    cut into small dice
2 medium potatoes, peeled and
    cut into small pieces
175 g/6 oz/1⅓ cups plain/all-purpose flour
300 ml/½ pt/1¼ cups fish or vegetable stock
2 tbsp whipping cream
1 tsp freshly chopped dill

FOR THE CRUMBLE TOPPING:
75 g/3 oz/⅓ cup butter or margarine
175 g/6 oz/1⅓ cups plain/all-purpose flour
75 g/3 oz/¾ cup Parmesan cheese, grated
¾ tsp cayenne pepper

 Preheat the oven to 200°C/400°F/Gas Mark 6, 15 minutes before cooking. Oil a 1.4l/2½ pt pie dish. Place the fish in a saucepan with the milk, salt and pepper. Bring to the boil, cover and simmer for 8–10 minutes until the fish is cooked. Remove with a slotted spoon, reserving the cooking liquid. Flake the fish into the prepared dish.

 Heat the oil and 1 tablespoon of the butter or margarine in a small frying pan and gently fry the onion, leeks, carrot and potatoes for 1–2 minutes. Cover tightly and cook over a gentle heat for a further 10 minutes until softened. Spoon the vegetables over the fish.

 Melt the remaining butter or margarine in a saucepan, add the flour and cook for 1 minute, stirring. Whisk in the reserved cooking liquid and the stock. Cook until thickened, then stir in the cream. Remove from the heat and stir in the dill. Pour over the fish.

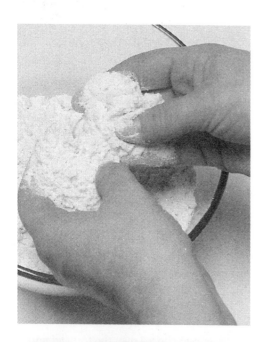

 To make the crumble, rub the butter or margarine into the flour until it resembles breadcrumbs, then stir in the cheese and cayenne pepper. Sprinkle over the dish and bake in the preheated oven for 20 minutes until piping hot.

Tasty Tip

Vary the taste and texture of the topping by making it with wholemeal/whole-wheat flour, or by adding 25 g/1 oz/¼ cup chopped nuts or jumbo porridge oats.

Supreme Baked Potatoes

Ingredients (Serves 4)

4 large baking potatoes
3 tbsp butter
1 tbsp sunflower oil
1 carrot, peeled and chopped
2 celery stalks, trimmed and finely chopped
200 g/7 oz can white crabmeat
2 spring onions/scallions, trimmed and finely chopped
salt and freshly ground black pepper
50 g/2 oz/½ cup Cheddar cheese, grated
tomato salad, to serve

Preheat the oven to 200°C/400°F/Gas Mark 6. Scrub the potatoes and prick all over with a fork, or thread 2 potatoes on to 2 long metal skewers. Place the potatoes in the preheated oven for 1–1½ hours, or until soft to the touch. Allow to cool a little, then cut in half.

Scoop out the cooked potato and turn into a bowl, leaving a reasonably firm potato shell. Mash the cooked potato flesh, then mix in the butter and mash until the butter has melted.

While the potatoes are cooking, heat the oil in a frying pan and cook the carrot and celery for 2 minutes. Cover the pan tightly and continue to cook for another 5 minutes, or until the vegetables are tender.

Add the cooked vegetables to the bowl of mashed potato and mix well. Fold in the crabmeat and the spring onions, then season to taste with salt and pepper.

Pile the mixture back into the potato shells and press in firmly. Sprinkle the grated cheese over the top and return the potato halves to the oven for 12–15 minutes until hot, golden and bubbling. Serve immediately with a tomato salad.

Tasty Tip

Threading the potatoes on to metal skewers helps them to cook more evenly and quickly as heat is transferred via the metal to the centres of the potatoes during cooking. To give the skins a crunchier finish, rub them with a little oil and lightly sprinkle with salt before baking.

Tuna Cannelloni

Ingredients (Serves 4)

1 tbsp olive oil
6 spring onions/scallions, trimmed and finely sliced
1 sweet Mediterranean red pepper/bell pepper,
  deseeded and finely chopped
200 g/7 oz can tuna in brine
250 g/9 oz tub ricotta or quark cheese
zest and juice of 1 lemon
1 tbsp freshly snipped chives
salt and freshly ground black pepper
8 dried cannelloni tubes
1 medium/large egg, beaten
125 g/4 oz/¼ cup cottage cheese
150 ml/¼ pt/⅔ cup natural/plain yoghurt
pinch of freshly grated nutmeg
50 g/2 oz/¼ cup mozzarella cheese, grated
tossed green salad, to serve

 Preheat the oven to 180°C/375°F/Gas Mark 5, 10 minutes before cooking. Heat the olive oil in a frying pan and cook the spring onions and pepper until soft. Remove from the pan with a slotted draining spoon and place in a large bowl.

 Drain the tuna, then stir into the spring onions and pepper. Beat the ricotta cheese with the lemon zest and juice and the snipped chives and season to taste with salt and pepper until soft and blended. Add to the tuna and mix together. If the mixture is still a little stiff, add a little extra lemon juice.

 With a teaspoon, carefully spoon the mixture into the cannelloni tubes, then lay the filled tubes in a lightly oiled shallow ovenproof dish. Beat the egg, cottage cheese, yoghurt and nutmeg together and pour over the cannelloni. Sprinkle with the grated mozzarella cheese and bake in the preheated oven for 15–20 minutes, or until the topping is golden brown and bubbling. Serve immediately with a tossed green salad.

Helpful Hint

It may seem tempting to part cook the cannelloni tubes before stuffing them, but this makes them too slippery to handle. The moisture in the sauce is sufficient to cook them thoroughly while they are baking in the oven.

Fried Fish with Thai Chilli Dipping Sauce

Ingredients (Serves 4)

1 large/extra-large egg white
½ tsp curry powder or turmeric
3–4 tbsp cornflour/cornstarch
salt and freshly ground black pepper
4 plaice/flounder or sole fillets, about 225 g/8 oz each
300 ml/½ pt/1¼ cups vegetable oil

FOR THE DIPPING SAUCE:
2 red chillies, deseeded and thinly sliced
2 shallots, peeled and finely chopped
1 tbsp freshly squeezed lime juice
3 tbsp Thai fish sauce
1 tbsp freshly chopped coriander/cilantro or Thai basil

TO SERVE:
freshly cooked rice
mixed salad leaves

To make the dipping sauce, combine all the ingredients in a bowl. Leave for at least 15 minutes.

Beat the egg white until frothy and whisk into a shallow dish.

Stir the curry powder or turmeric into the cornflour in a bowl and season to taste with salt and pepper. Dip each fish fillet in the beaten egg white, dust lightly on both sides with the cornflour mixture and place on a wire rack.

Heat a wok or large frying pan, add the oil and heat to 180°C/350°F. Add 1 or 2 fillets and fry for 5 minutes, or until crisp and golden, turning once during cooking.

Using a slotted spatula, carefully remove the cooked fish and drain on absorbent kitchen paper. Keep warm while frying the remaining fillets.

Arrange the fillets on warmed individual plates and serve immediately with the dipping sauce, rice and salad.

Helpful Hint

To prepare fresh chillies, slit them lengthways with a small sharp knife, then remove and discard the seeds, unless you want a really fiery dish. Wash your hands thoroughly with soap and water as the volatile oils can cause irritation.

Sardines with Redcurrants

Ingredients (Serves 4)

2 tbsp redcurrant jelly
finely grated zest of 1 lime
2 tbsp medium dry sherry
450 g/1 lb fresh sardines, cleaned and heads removed
sea salt and freshly ground black pepper
fresh green salad, to serve

TO GARNISH:
fresh redcurrants
lime wedges

☑ Preheat the grill/broiler and line the grill rack with kitchen foil 2–3 minutes before cooking.

☑ Warm the redcurrant jelly in a bowl standing over a pan of gently simmering water and stir until smooth. Add the lime zest and sherry to the bowl and stir well until blended.

☑ Lightly rinse the sardines and pat dry with absorbent kitchen paper. Place on a chopping board and, with a sharp knife, make several diagonal cuts across the flesh of each fish.

☑ Season the sardines inside the cavities with salt and pepper, then gently brush the warm marinade over the skin and inside the cavities.

☑ Place on the grill/broiler rack and cook under the preheated grill for 8–10 minutes, or until the fish are cooked.

☑ Carefully turn the sardines over at least once during grilling. Baste occasionally with the remaining redcurrant and lime marinade. Serve immediately with the salad and garnish with the redcurrants and lime wedges.

Handy Hint
Most fish are sold cleaned but it is easy to do yourself. Using the back of a knife, scrape off the scales from the tail towards the head. Make a small slit along their bellies using a sharp knife. Carefully scrape out the entrails and rinse thoroughly under cold running water. Pat dry with absorbent paper.

Saucy Cod and Pasta Bake

Ingredients (Serves 4)

450 g/1 lb cod or firm white fish fillets, skinned
2 tbsp sunflower oil
1 onion, peeled and chopped
4 rashers smoked streaky bacon, rind removed,
   and chopped
150 g/5 oz/1½ cups baby button mushrooms, wiped
2 celery stalks, trimmed and thinly sliced
2 small courgettes/zucchini, halved lengthways
   and sliced
400 g/14 oz can chopped tomatoes
100 ml/3½ fl oz/⅓ cup fish stock or dry white wine
1 tbsp freshly chopped tarragon
salt and freshly ground black pepper

FOR THE PASTA TOPPING:
225–275 g/8–10 oz/2–2½ cups pasta shells
2 tbsp butter
4 tbsp plain/all-purpose flour
450 ml/¾ pt/1¾ cups milk

 Preheat the oven to 200°C/400°F/Gas Mark 6, 15 minutes before cooking. Cut the cod into bite-size pieces and reserve.

 Heat the sunflower oil in a large saucepan, add the onion and bacon and cook for 7–8 minutes. Add the mushrooms and celery and cook for 5 minutes, or until fairly soft.

Add the courgettes and tomatoes to the bacon mixture and pour in the fish stock or wine. Bring to the boil, then simmer uncovered for 5 minutes, or until the sauce has thickened slightly. Remove from the heat and stir in the cod pieces and the tarragon. Season to taste with salt and pepper, then spoon into a large oiled baking dish.

Meanwhile, bring a large pan of lightly salted water to a rolling boil. Add the pasta shells and cook, according to the packet instructions, or until *al dente*.

For the topping, place the butter and flour in a saucepan and pour in the milk. Bring to the boil slowly, whisking until thickened and smooth.

Drain the pasta thoroughly and stir into the sauce. Spoon carefully over the fish and vegetables. Place in the preheated oven and bake for 20–25 minutes, or until the top is lightly browned and bubbling.

Helpful Hint

If you are short of time, you can make a simpler topping. Beat together 2 eggs, 3 tablespoons Greek-style/plain yoghurt and 3 tablespoons double/heavy cream; season to taste with salt and pepper. Add the drained pasta and mix well. Spoon on top of the fish and vegetables and bake as above for 15–20 minutes, or until the top is set and golden brown.

Recipes: Meat & Poultry

PACKED WITH
MONEY
SAVING
• IDEAS & TIPS •

Spaghetti Bolognese

Ingredients (Serves 4)

3 tbsp olive oil
50 g/2 oz/¼ cup unsmoked streaky bacon,
    rind removed, and chopped
1 small onion, peeled and finely chopped
1 carrot, peeled and finely chopped
1 celery stick, trimmed and finely chopped
2 garlic cloves, peeled and crushed
1 bay leaf
500 g/1 lb 2 oz/5¼ cups minced/ground beef steak
400 g/14 oz can chopped tomatoes
2 tbsp tomato paste
150 ml/¼ pt/⅔ cup red wine
150 ml/¼ pt/⅔ cup beef stock
salt and freshly ground black pepper
450 g/1 lb spaghetti
freshly grated Parmesan cheese, to serve

 Heat the olive oil in a large, heavy-based pan, add the bacon and cook for 5 minutes, or until slightly coloured. Add the onion, carrot, celery, garlic and bay leaf and cook, stirring, for 8 minutes, or until the vegetables are soft.

 Add the beef to the pan and cook, stirring with a wooden spoon to break up any lumps in the meat, for 5-8 minutes, or until browned.

 Stir the tomatoes and tomato paste into the mince and pour in the wine and stock. Bring to the boil, lower the heat and simmer for at least 40 minutes, stirring occasionally. The longer you leave the sauce to cook, the more intense the flavour. Season to taste with salt and pepper and remove the bay leaf.

 Meanwhile, bring a large pan of lightly salted water to a rolling boil, add the spaghetti and cook for about 8 minutes or until *al dente*. Drain and arrange on warmed serving plates. Top with the prepared bolognese sauce and serve immediately, sprinkled with grated Parmesan cheese.

Budget Tip

If necessary, replace the wine with more stock and add a dash of Worcester sauce, to taste. Bolognese sauce is a classic base for the meat sauce used in a lasagne.

Colourful Beef in Lettuce

Ingredients (Serves 4)

450 g/1 lb fresh minced/ground beef
2 tbsp Chinese rice wine
1 tbsp light soy sauce
2 tsp sesame oil
2 tsp cornflour/cornstarch
25 g/1 oz/1 cup Chinese dried mushrooms
2 tbsp groundnut/peanut oil
1 garlic clove, peeled and crushed
1 shallot, peeled and finely chopped
2 spring onions/scallions, trimmed and finely sliced
2 carrots, peeled and cut into matchsticks
125 g/4 oz/½ cup canned bamboo shoots, drained
    and cut into matchsticks
2 courgettes/zucchini, trimmed and cut into matchsticks
1 red pepper/bell pepper, deseeded and cut
    into matchsticks
1 tbsp dark soy sauce
2 tbsp hoisin sauce
2 tbsp oyster sauce
4 large iceberg lettuce leaves
sprigs of fresh flat-leaf parsley, to garnish

Place the minced beef in a bowl with 1 tablespoon of the Chinese rice wine, the light soy sauce, sesame oil and cornflour. Mix well and leave for 20 minutes.

Soak the dried mushrooms in almost boiling water for 20 minutes. Drain, rinse, drain again and squeeze out excess liquid. Trim and slice finely.

Heat a wok or large frying pan, add 1 tablespoon of the groundnut/peanut oil and, when very hot, add the beef.

Stir-fry for 1 minute, then, using a slotted spoon, remove. Reserve.

Wipe the wok clean and reheat. Add the remaining oil and, when hot, add the garlic, shallot and spring onions and stir-fry for 10 seconds. Add the carrots and stir-fry for 1 minute. Add the mushrooms with the bamboo shoots, courgettes and pepper and stir-fry for 1 minute. Add the reserved beef, soy, hoisin and oyster sauces to the wok and stir-fry for 3 minutes.

Spoon the beef mixture on to the lettuce leaves and fold into parcels. Garnish with flat-leaf parsley and serve.

Helpful Hint
If you can afford it, use a good-quality meat for this dish, such as steak mince, and fry over a high heat so that it browns well.

Steak and Kidney Stew

Ingredients (Serves 4)

1 tbsp olive oil
1 onion, peeled and chopped
2–3 garlic cloves, peeled and crushed
2 celery stalks, trimmed and sliced
550 g/1¼ lb braising steak, trimmed and diced
125 g/4 oz lambs' kidneys, cored and chopped
2 tbsp plain/all-purpose flour
1 tbsp tomato puree/paste
900 ml/1½ pts/scant 1 qt beef stock
salt and freshly ground black pepper
1 fresh bay leaf
300 g/10 oz/2⅓ cups carrots, peeled and sliced
350 g/12 oz baby new potatoes, scrubbed
350 g/12 oz/6 cups fresh spinach leaves, chopped

FOR THE DUMPLINGS:
125 g/4 oz/¾ cup self-raising flour
50 g/2 oz/⅖ cup shredded suet/lard
1 tbsp freshly chopped mixed herbs
2–3 tbsp water

 Heat the oil in a large, heavy-based saucepan, add the onion, garlic and celery and sauté for 5 minutes, or until browned. Remove from the pan with a slotted spoon and reserve.

Add the steak and kidneys to the pan and cook for 3–5 minutes, or until sealed, then return the onion mixture to the pan. Sprinkle in the flour and cook, stirring, for 2 minutes. Take off the heat, stir in the tomato puree, then the stock, and season to taste with salt and pepper. Add the bay leaf.

Return to the heat and bring to the boil, stirring occasionally. Add the carrots, then reduce the heat to a simmer and cover with a lid. Cook for 1¼ hours, stirring occasionally. Reduce the heat if the liquid is evaporating quickly. Add the potatoes and cook for a further 30 minutes.

Place the flour, suet and herbs in a bowl and add a little seasoning. Add the water and mix to a stiff mixture. Using a little extra flour, shape into 8 small balls. Place the dumplings on top of the stew, cover with the lid and continue to cook for 15 minutes, or until the meat is tender and the dumplings are well risen and fluffy. Stir in the spinach and leave to stand for 2 minutes, or until the spinach has wilted.

Budget Tip

As it uses braising steak and kidneys, this is a great way of creating a tasty, rich meat dish without having to use expensive meat cuts.

Leek and Ham Risotto

Ingredients (Serves 4)

1 tbsp olive oil
2 tbsp butter
1 medium onion, peeled and finely chopped
4 leeks, trimmed and thinly sliced
1½ tbsp freshly chopped thyme
350 g/12 oz Arborio rice
1.4 l/2¼ pts/5½ cups vegetable or chicken
    stock, heated
225 g/8 oz/1¼ cup cooked ham
175 g/6 oz/1¼ cup peas, thawed if frozen
50 g/2 oz/½ cup Parmesan cheese, grated
salt and freshly ground black pepper

 Heat the oil and half the butter together in a large saucepan. Add the onion and leeks and cook over a medium heat for 6–8 minutes, stirring occasionally, until soft and beginning to colour. Stir in the thyme and cook briefly.

 Add the rice and stir well. Continue stirring over a medium heat for about 1 minute until the rice is glossy. Add a ladleful or two of the stock and stir well until the stock is absorbed. Continue adding stock, a ladleful at a time, and stirring well between additions, until about two-thirds of the stock has been added. (Risotto should take about 15 minutes to cook, so taste it after this time – the rice should be creamy with just a slight bite to it. If it is not quite ready, continue adding the stock, a little at a time, and cook for a few more minutes. Stop as soon as it tastes ready as you do not have to add all of the liquid.)

 Meanwhile, either chop or finely shred the ham, then add to the saucepan of rice, together with the peas. Continue adding ladlefuls of stock, as described in step 2, until the rice is tender and the ham is heated through thoroughly.

 Add the remaining butter, sprinkle over the Parmesan cheese and season to taste with salt and pepper. When the butter has melted and the cheese has softened, stir well to incorporate. Taste and adjust the seasoning, then serve immediately.

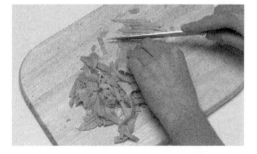

Chinese Fried Rice

Ingredients (Serves 4)

450 g/1 lb/2 cups long-grain rice
2 tbsp groundnut/peanut oil
50 g/2 oz/¼ cup smoked bacon, chopped
2 garlic cloves, peeled and finely chopped
1 tsp freshly grated root ginger
125 g/4 oz/1 cup frozen peas, thawed
2 medium/large eggs, beaten
125 g/4 oz/¾ cup bean sprouts
salt and freshly ground black pepper

TO GARNISH:
50 g/2 oz/½ cup roasted peanuts, chopped
3 spring onions/scallions, trimmed and finely chopped

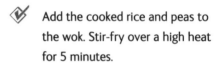 Wash the rice in several changes of water until it runs relatively clear. Drain well. Put into a saucepan or flameproof casserole dish with a tight-fitting lid. Pour in enough water to cover the rice by about 1 cm/½ in. Add salt and bring to the boil. As soon as the water boils, cover the saucepan, reduce the heat as low as possible and cook for 10 minutes. Remove from the heat and leave to stand for a further 10 minutes. Do not lift the lid while cooking. Leave until cold, then stir with a fork.

Heat a wok, add the oil and, when hot, add the smoked bacon. Stir-fry for 1 minute before adding the garlic and ginger, then stir-fry for a further 30 seconds.

Add the cooked rice and peas to the wok. Stir-fry over a high heat for 5 minutes.

Add the eggs and the bean sprouts and continue to stir-fry for a further 2 minutes until the eggs have set. Season to taste with salt and pepper. Spoon the mixture on to a serving plate and garnish with the peanuts and spring onions. Serve hot or cold.

Tasty Tip
This dish is an excellent accompaniment to plain grilled chicken or fish or to serve with any meat that has been marinated with Chinese flavours.

Cannelloni

Ingredients (Serves 4)

2 tbsp olive oil
175 g/6 oz/³⁄₄ cup fresh minced/ground pork
75 g/3 oz/²⁄₃ cup chicken livers, chopped
1 small onion, peeled and chopped
1 garlic clove, peeled and chopped
175 g/6 oz/1 cup frozen spinach, thawed and chopped
1 tbsp freeze-dried oregano
pinch of freshly grated nutmeg
salt and freshly ground black pepper
175 g/6 oz/³⁄₄ cup ricotta or quark cheese
25 g/1 oz/¹⁄₄ stick butter
25 g/1 oz/¹⁄₄ cup plain/all-purpose flour
600 ml/1 pt/2¹⁄₂ cups milk
600 ml/1 pt/2¹⁄₂ cups ready-made tomato sauce
16 precooked cannelloni tubes
50 g/2 oz/¹⁄₂ cup Parmesan cheese, grated
green salad, to serve

Preheat the oven to 190°C/375°F/Gas Mark 5, 10 minutes before cooking. Heat the olive oil in a frying pan and cook the pork and chicken livers for about 5 minutes, stirring occasionally, until browned all over. Break up any lumps with a wooden spoon.

Add the onion and garlic and cook for 4 minutes, until softened. Add the spinach, oregano and nutmeg and season to taste with salt and pepper. Cook until all the liquid has evaporated, then remove the pan from the heat and allow to cool. Stir in the ricotta or quark cheese.

Meanwhile, melt the butter in a small saucepan and stir in the plain flour to form a roux. Cook for 2 minutes, stirring occasionally. Remove from the heat and blend in the milk until smooth. Return to the heat and bring to the boil, stirring until the sauce has thickened. Reserve.

Spoon a thin layer of the tomato sauce on the base of a large ovenproof dish. Divide the pork filling between the cannelloni tubes. Arrange on top of the tomato sauce. Spoon over the remaining tomato sauce.

 Pour over the white sauce and sprinkle with the Parmesan cheese. Bake in the preheated oven for 30–35 minutes, or until the cannelloni is tender and the top is golden brown. Serve immediately with a green salad.

Tasty Tip
To make chicken cannelloni, substitute 225 g/8 oz boneless, skinless chicken breast that has been finely chopped in a food processor. Minced chicken is also available from large supermarkets.

Oven-roasted Vegetables with Sausages

Ingredients (Serves 4)

2 medium aubergines/eggplants, trimmed
3 medium courgettes/zucchini, trimmed
4 tbsp olive oil
6 garlic cloves
8 Tuscany-style sausages
4 plum tomatoes
2 x 325 g/11 oz cans cannellini beans
salt and freshly ground black pepper
1 bunch fresh basil, torn into coarse pieces
4 tbsp Parmesan cheese, grated

Preheat the oven to 200°C/400°F/Gas Mark 6, 15 minutes before cooking. Cut the aubergines and courgettes into bite-size chunks. Place the olive oil in a large roasting tin and heat in the preheated oven for 3 minutes, or until very hot. Add the aubergines, courgettes and garlic cloves, then stir until coated in the hot oil and cook in the oven for 10 minutes.

Remove the roasting tin from the oven and stir. Lightly prick the sausages, add to the roasting tin and return to the oven. Continue to roast for a further 20 minutes, turning once during cooking, until the vegetables are tender and the sausages are golden brown.

Meanwhile, roughly chop the plum tomatoes and drain the cannellini beans. Remove the sausages from the oven and stir in the tomatoes and cannellini beans. Season to taste with salt and pepper, then return to the oven for 5 minutes, or until heated thoroughly.

Scatter over the basil leaves and sprinkle with plenty of Parmesan cheese and extra freshly ground black pepper. Serve immediately.

Helpful Hint

Although it is worth seeking out Tuscany-style sausages for this dish, a good alternative would be to use Toulouse sausages instead, as these are more readily available from large supermarkets and from selected butchers. Or use the best quality sausage you can afford.

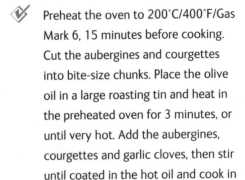

Lancashire Hotpot

Ingredients (Serves 4)

1 kg/2¼ lb middle end neck of lamb, divided
  into cutlets
2 tbsp vegetable oil
2 large onions, peeled and sliced
2 tsp plain/all-purpose flour
150 ml/¼ pt/⅔ cup vegetable or lamb stock
700 g/1½ lb/3¼ cups waxy potatoes, peeled
  and thickly sliced
salt and freshly ground black pepper
1 bay leaf
2 sprigs fresh thyme
1 tbsp melted butter
2 tbsp freshly chopped herbs, to garnish
freshly cooked green beans, to serve

Preheat the oven to 170°C/325°F/Gas Mark 3. Trim any excess fat from the lamb cutlets. Heat the oil in a frying pan and brown the cutlets in batches for 3–4 minutes. Remove with a slotted spoon and reserve.

Add the onions to the frying pan and cook for 6–8 minutes until softened and just beginning to colour, then remove and reserve. Stir in the flour and cook for a few seconds, then gradually pour in the stock, stirring well, and bring to the boil. Remove from the heat.

Spread the base of a large casserole dish with half the potato slices. Top with half the onions and season well with salt and pepper. Arrange the browned meat in a layer. Season again and add the remaining onions, bay leaf and thyme. Pour in the stock mixture and top with remaining potatoes so that they overlap in a single layer. Brush the potatoes with the melted butter and season again.

Cover the saucepan and cook in the preheated oven for 2 hours, uncovering for the last 30 minutes to allow the potatoes to brown. Garnish with chopped herbs and serve immediately with green beans.

Budget Tip
It is important to season the lamb well and to cook it slowly, so that it is meltingly tender – you will see that cheaper cuts of meat can be some of the tastiest.

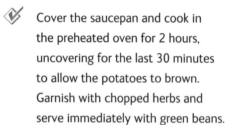

Lamb and Potato Moussaka

Ingredients (Serves 4)

700 g/1½ lb cooked roast lamb
700 g/1½ lb potatoes, peeled
125 g/4 oz/1 stick butter
1 large onion, peeled and chopped
2–4 garlic cloves, peeled and crushed
3 tbsp tomato puree/paste
1 tbsp freshly chopped parsley
salt and freshly ground black pepper
3–4 tbsp olive oil
2 medium aubergines/eggplants, trimmed and sliced
4 medium tomatoes, sliced
2 medium/large eggs
300 ml/½ pt/1¼ cups Greek/plain yoghurt
2–3 tbsp Parmesan cheese, grated

Preheat the oven to 200°C/400°F/Gas Mark 6, about 15 minutes before required. Trim the lamb, discarding any fat, then cut into fine dice and reserve. Thinly slice the potatoes and rinse thoroughly in cold water, then pat dry with a clean tea towel.

Melt 3 tablespoons of the butter in a frying pan and fry the potatoes, in batches, until crisp and golden.

Using a slotted spoon, remove from the pan and reserve. Use a third of the potatoes to line the base of an ovenproof dish.

Add the onion and garlic to the butter remaining in the pan and cook for 5 minutes. Add the lamb and fry for 1 minute. Blend the tomato puree with 3 tablespoons water and stir into the pan with the parsley and salt and pepper. Spoon over the layer of potatoes, then top with the remaining potato slices.

Heat the oil and the remaining butter in the pan and brown the aubergine slices for 5–6 minutes. Arrange the tomatoes on top of the potatoes, then the aubergines on top of the tomatoes. Beat the eggs with the yoghurt and Parmesan and pour over the aubergine and tomatoes. Bake in the preheated oven for 25 minutes, or until golden and piping hot. Serve.

Budget Tip

This is a good way to use up leftover lamb. Or you could brown some minced/ground lamb in a pan instead.

Lamb Meatballs with Savoy Cabbage

Ingredients (Serves 4)

450 g/1 lb fresh minced/ground lamb
1 tbsp freshly chopped parsley
1 tbsp freshly grated root ginger
1 tbsp light soy sauce
1 medium/large egg yolk
4 tbsp dark soy sauce
2 tbsp dry sherry
1 tbsp cornflour/cornstarch
3 tbsp vegetable oil
2 garlic cloves, peeled and chopped
1 bunch spring onions/scallions, trimmed and shredded
½ Savoy cabbage, trimmed and shredded
½ head Chinese leaves, trimmed and shredded
freshly chopped red chilli, to garnish

 Place the lamb in a large bowl with the parsley, ginger, light soy sauce and egg yolk and mix together. Divide the mixture into walnut-size pieces and, using your hands, roll into balls. Place on a baking sheet, cover with clingfilm/plastic wrap and chill in the refrigerator for at least 30 minutes.

Meanwhile, blend together the dark soy sauce, sherry and cornflour with 2 tablespoons water in a small bowl until smooth. Reserve.

Heat a wok, add the oil and, when hot, add the meatballs and cook for 5–8 minutes, or until browned all over, turning occasionally. Using a slotted spoon, transfer the meatballs to a large plate and keep warm.

Add the garlic, spring onions, Savoy cabbage and Chinese leaves to the wok and stir-fry for 3 minutes. Pour over the reserved soy sauce mixture, bring to the boil, then simmer for 30 seconds, or until thickened. Return the meatballs to the wok and mix in. Garnish with chopped red chilli and serve immediately.

Tasty Tip
This dish is made with simple, basic ingredients, but you can substitute more Chinese ingredients if you prefer, such as rice wine vinegar instead of sherry and pak choi/bok choy leaves instead of Savoy cabbage.

Slow-roast Chicken with Potatoes and Oregano

Ingredients (Serves 6)

1.4–1.8 kg/3–4 lb oven-ready chicken, preferably
   free range
1 lemon, halved
1 onion, peeled and quartered
50 g/2 oz/¼ cup butter, softened
salt and freshly ground black pepper
1 kg/2¼ lb potatoes, peeled and quartered
3–4 tbsp extra virgin olive oil
1 tbsp dried oregano, crumbled
1 tsp fresh thyme leaves
2 tbsp freshly chopped thyme
fresh sage leaves, to garnish

Preheat the oven to 200°C/400°F/Gas Mark 6. Rinse the chicken and dry well, inside and out, with absorbent kitchen paper. Rub the chicken all over with the lemon halves, then squeeze the juice over it and into the cavity. Put the squeezed halves into the cavity with the quartered onion.

Rub the softened butter all over the chicken and season to taste with salt and pepper, then put it in a large roasting tin, breast-side down.

Toss the potatoes in the oil, season with salt and pepper to taste and add the dried oregano and fresh thyme. Arrange the potatoes with the oil around the chicken and carefully pour 150 ml/¼ pt/⅔ cup water into one end of the pan (not over the oil).

Roast in the preheated oven for 25 minutes. Reduce the oven temperature to 190°C/375°F/Gas Mark 5 and turn the chicken breast-side up. Turn the potatoes, sprinkle

Budget Tip
Roast chicken is a popular family meal that does not need to be sacrificed in these hard times – a whole chicken can be much more economical than buying prime breast cuts as you get much more for your money. And do not forget that you can use any leftovers in sandwiches and other meals, and use the carcass to make home-made stock.

 Carve the chicken into serving pieces and arrange on a large heatproof serving dish. Arrange the potatoes around the chicken and drizzle over any remaining juices. Sprinkle with the remaining herbs and serve.

over half the fresh herbs and baste the chicken and potatoes with the juices. Continue roasting for 1 hour, or until the chicken is cooked, basting occasionally. If the liquid evaporates completely, add a little more water. The chicken is done when the juices run clear when the thigh is pierced with a skewer.

 Transfer the chicken to a carving board and rest for 5 minutes, covered with kitchen foil. Return the potatoes to the oven while the chicken is resting.

Tasty Tip

Roasting the chicken breast-side down for the first 25 minutes of cooking allows the fat and juices to run into the breast, keeping it moist. It is important to baste the chicken now and then, once it is turned, so that the breast does not dry out.

Cheesy Baked Chicken Macaroni

Ingredients (Serves 4)

1 tbsp olive oil
350 g/12 oz/3¼ cups boneless, skinless chicken
   breasts, diced
75 g/3 oz/⅓ cup pancetta, diced
1 onion, peeled and chopped
1 garlic clove, peeled and chopped
350 g packet/1½ cups fresh tomato sauce
400 g/14 oz can chopped tomatoes
2 tbsp freshly chopped basil, plus leaves to garnish
salt and freshly ground black pepper
350 g/12 oz/3 cups macaroni
150 g/5 oz/1¼ cups mozzarella cheese,
   drained and chopped
50 g/2 oz/½ cup Gruyère cheese, grated
50 g/2 oz/½ cup freshly grated Parmesan cheese

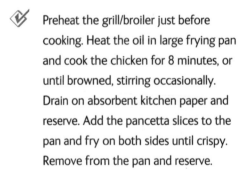

Preheat the grill/broiler just before cooking. Heat the oil in large frying pan and cook the chicken for 8 minutes, or until browned, stirring occasionally. Drain on absorbent kitchen paper and reserve. Add the pancetta slices to the pan and fry on both sides until crispy. Remove from the pan and reserve.

Add the onion and garlic to the frying pan and cook for 5 minutes, or until softened. Stir in the tomato sauce, chopped tomatoes and basil and season to taste with salt and pepper. Bring to the boil, lower the heat and simmer the sauce for 5 minutes.

Meanwhile, bring a large pan of lightly salted water to a rolling boil. Add the macaroni and cook according to the packet instructions, or until *al dente*.

Drain the macaroni thoroughly, return to the pan and stir in the sauce, chicken and mozzarella cheese. Spoon into a shallow ovenproof dish.

Sprinkle the pancetta over the macaroni. Sprinkle over the Gruyère and Parmesan cheeses. Place under the preheated grill and cook for 5–10 minutes, or until golden brown; turn the dish occasionally. Garnish and serve immediately.

Budget Tip
You could always substitute bacon for the pancetta, and use Cheddar instead of the Gruyère and Parmesan cheeses.

Lemon Chicken

Ingredients (Serves 4)

450 g/1 lb skinless, boneless chicken
  breast fillets, cubed
1 medium/large egg white, beaten
1 tsp salt
1 tbsp sesame oil
1 tbsp cornflour/cornstarch
200 ml/7 fl oz/³/₄ cup groundnut/peanut oil
75 ml/3 fl oz/6 tbsp chicken stock
zest and juice of 1 lemon
1 tbsp caster/superfine sugar
1 tbsp light soy sauce
2 tbsp Chinese rice wine or dry sherry
3 large garlic cloves, peeled and finely chopped
1–2 tsp dried red chillies, crushed
shredded fresh red chillies, to garnish
freshly steamed white rice, to serve

 Place the cubes of chicken in a large bowl, then add the beaten egg white, salt, 1 teaspoon of the sesame oil and 1 teaspoon of the cornflour. Mix lightly together until all the chicken is coated, then chill in the refrigerator for 20 minutes.

 Heat the wok until very hot and add the oil. When hot, remove the wok from the heat and add the chicken. Stir-fry for 2 minutes, or until the chicken turns white, then remove with a slotted spoon and drain on absorbent kitchen paper.

 Wipe the wok clean and heat it until hot again. Add the stock, lemon zest and juice, sugar, soy sauce, Chinese rice wine or sherry, garlic and crushed chillies and bring to the boil. Blend the remaining cornflour to a smooth paste with 1 tablespoon water and add to the wok. Stir, then simmer for 1 minute. Add the chicken cubes and stir-fry for 2–3 minutes. Add the remaining sesame oil, garnish with shredded chillies and serve immediately with freshly steamed rice.

Budget Tip

Chicken thighs, or using turkey instead of chicken, may prove to be cheaper than chicken breast fillets, and yet just as delicious.

Turkey and Mixed Mushroom Lasagne

Ingredients (Serves 4)

1 tbsp olive oil
225 g/8 oz/2 cups mixed mushrooms e.g. button,
 chestnut and portobello, wiped and sliced
15 g/¹/₂ oz/1 tbsp butter
25 g/1 oz/¹/₄ cup plain/all-purpose flour
300 ml/¹/₂ pt/1¹/₄ cups skimmed/non-fat milk
1 bay leaf
225 g/8 oz/1¹/₂ cups cooked turkey, cubed
¹/₄ tsp freshly grated nutmeg
salt and freshly ground black pepper
400 g/14 oz can plum tomatoes, drained and chopped
1 tsp dried mixed herbs
9 lasagne sheets (about 150 g/5 oz)

FOR THE TOPPING:
200 ml/7 fl oz/³/₄ cup low-fat Greek/plain yoghurt
1 medium/large egg, lightly beaten
1 tbsp finely grated Parmesan cheese
mixed salad leaves, to serve

Preheat the oven to 180°C/350°F/
Gas Mark 4. Heat the oil and cook
the mushrooms until tender and
all the juices have evaporated.
Remove and reserve.

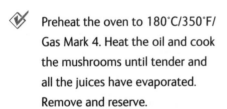

Put the butter, flour, milk and bay leaf
in the pan. Slowly bring to the boil,
stirring until thickened. Simmer for
2–3 minutes. Remove the bay leaf
and stir in the mushrooms, turkey,
nutmeg, salt and pepper.

Mix together the tomatoes and
mixed herbs and season with salt and
pepper. Spoon half into the base of
a 1.7 l/3 pt ovenproof dish. Top with
3 sheets of lasagne, then with half
the turkey mixture. Repeat the layers,
then arrange the remaining 3 sheets
of pasta on top.

Mix together the yoghurt and egg.
Spoon over the lasagne, spreading
the mixture into the corners. Sprinkle
with the Parmesan and bake in the
preheated oven for 45 minutes.
Serve with the mixed salad.

Tasty Tip

Garlic bread is the perfect
accompaniment to lasagne. Preheat the
oven at 180°C/350°F/Gas Mark 4. Finely
chop 2–3 garlic cloves. Mix with a little
chopped parsley and 125 g/4 oz/1 stick
butter or low-fat spread. Make cuts
almost to the base of a French stick.
Spread with the flavoured butter.
Wrap in kitchen foil. Cook in the
preheated oven for 15 minutes.

Recipes: Vegetables

PACKED WITH • MONEY SAVING • IDEAS & TIPS

Vegetarian Spaghetti Bolognese

Ingredients (Serves 4)

2 tbsp olive oil
1 onion, peeled and finely chopped
1 carrot, peeled and finely chopped
1 celery stalk, trimmed and finely chopped
225 g/8 oz Quorn mince/soy meat substitute
150 ml/¼ pt/⅔ cup red wine
300 ml/½ pt/1¼ cups vegetable stock
1 tsp mushroom ketchup
4 tbsp tomato puree/paste
350 g/12 oz/4 cups dried spaghetti
4 tbsp half/reduced fat crème fraîche/sour cream
salt and freshly ground black pepper
1 tbsp freshly chopped parsley

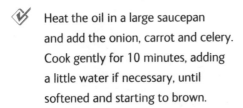

Heat the oil in a large saucepan and add the onion, carrot and celery. Cook gently for 10 minutes, adding a little water if necessary, until softened and starting to brown.

Add the Quorn mince and cook for a further 2–3 minutes before adding the red wine. Increase the heat and simmer gently until nearly all the wine has evaporated.

Mix together the vegetable stock and mushroom ketchup and add about half to the Quorn mixture along with the tomato puree. Cover and simmer gently for about 45 minutes, adding the remaining stock as necessary.

Meanwhile, bring a large pan of salted water to the boil and add the spaghetti. Cook until *al dente*, or according to the packet instructions. Drain well. Remove the sauce from the heat, add the crème fraîche and season to taste with salt and pepper. Stir in the parsley and serve immediately with the pasta.

Helpful Hint
Quorn is a brand of foods made from mycoprotein, which is high in fibre and low in fat. It is derived from the mushroom family and readily takes on any flavour it is put with. An equivalent amount of minced/ground soya can be used in this recipe, whether dried (follow the packet instructions) or frozen.

Vegetable Cassoulet

Ingredients (Serves 6)

125 g/4 oz/²/₃ cup dried haricot or kidney beans,
    soaked overnight (or canned beans, if preferred)
2 tbsp olive oil
2 garlic cloves, peeled and chopped
9 baby onions, peeled and halved
2 carrots, peeled and diced
2 celery stalks, trimmed and finely chopped
1 red pepper/bell pepper, deseeded and chopped
175 g/6 oz/1¹/₂ cups mixed mushrooms, sliced
1 tbsp each freshly chopped rosemary,
    thyme and sage
150 ml/¹/₄ pt/²/₃ cup red wine
4 tbsp tomato puree/paste
1 tbsp dark soy sauce
salt and freshly ground black pepper
50 g/2 oz/¹/₂ cup fresh breadcrumbs
1 tbsp freshly chopped parsley
basil sprigs, to garnish

 Preheat the oven to 190°C/375°F/Gas Mark 5. Drain the beans and place in a saucepan with 1 l/1³/₄ pts/1 qt fresh water. Bring to the boil and boil rapidly for 10 minutes. Reduce the heat and simmer gently for 45 minutes. Drain the beans, reserving 300 ml/¹/₂ pt/1¹/₄ cups of the liquid.

 Heat 1 tablespoon of the oil in a flameproof casserole and add the garlic, onions, carrot, celery and red pepper. Cook gently for 10–12 minutes until tender and starting to brown. Add a little water if the vegetables start to stick. Add the mushrooms and cook for a further 5 minutes until softened. Add the herbs and stir briefly.

 Stir in the red wine and boil rapidly for about 5 minutes until reduced and syrupy. Stir in the reserved beans and their liquid, tomato puree and soy sauce. Season to taste with salt and pepper.

 Mix together the breadcrumbs and parsley with the remaining 1 table-spoon of oil. Scatter this mixture evenly over the top of the cassoulet. Cover loosely with foil and transfer to the preheated oven. Cook for 30 minutes. Carefully remove the foil and cook for a further 15–20 minutes until the topping is crisp and golden. Serve immediately, garnished with basil sprigs.

Mushroom Stew

Ingredients (Serves 4)

15 g/¹/₂ oz/¹/₄ cup dried porcini mushrooms
900 g/2 lb assorted fresh mushrooms, wiped
2 tbsp good quality virgin olive oil
1 onion, peeled and finely chopped
2 garlic cloves, peeled and finely chopped
1 tbsp fresh thyme leaves
pinch of ground cloves
salt and freshly ground black pepper
700 g/1¹/₂ lb tomatoes, peeled, deseeded and chopped
225 g/8 oz/2 cups instant polenta
600ml/1 pt/2¹/₂ cups vegetable stock
3 tbsp freshly chopped mixed herbs
sprigs of parsley, to garnish

Soak the porcini mushrooms
in a small bowl of hot water
for 20 minutes.

Drain, reserving the porcini
mushrooms and their soaking
liquid. Cut the fresh mushrooms
in half and reserve.

In a saucepan, heat the oil and
add the onion.

Cook gently for 5–7 minutes until
softened. Add the garlic, thyme
and cloves and continue cooking
for 2 minutes.

Add all the mushrooms and cook for
8–10 minutes until the mushrooms
have softened, stirring often.
Season to taste with salt and pepper
and add the tomatoes and the
reserved soaking liquid.

Simmer, partly-covered, over a
low heat for about 20 minutes
until thickened. Adjust the seasoning
to taste.

Meanwhile, cook the polenta according to the packet instructions, using the vegetable stock. Stir in the herbs and divide between 4 dishes.

Ladle the mushrooms over the polenta, garnish with the parsley and serve immediately.

Tasty Tip

For a dinner party version of this recipe, add a generous splash of red wine with the soaking liquid in step 5 and, just before serving, remove from the heat and stir in 2 tablespoons low-fat Greek/ plain yoghurt.

Light Ratatouille

Ingredients (Serves 4)

1 red pepper/bell pepper
2 courgettes/zucchini, trimmed
1 small aubergine/eggplant, trimmed
1 onion, peeled
2 ripe tomatoes
50 g/2 oz/1½ cups button mushrooms, wiped and halved or quartered
200 ml/7 fl oz/¾ cup tomato juice
1 tbsp freshly chopped basil
salt and freshly ground black pepper

Deseed the peppers, remove the membrane with a small sharp knife and cut into small dice. Thickly slice the courgettes and cut the aubergine into small dice. Slice the onion into rings.

Place the tomatoes in boiling water until their skins begin to peel away.

Remove the skins from the tomatoes, cut into quarters and remove the seeds.

Place all the vegetables in a saucepan with the tomato juice and basil. Season to taste with salt and pepper.

Bring to the boil, cover and simmer for 15 minutes, or until the vegetables are tender.

Remove the vegetables with a slotted spoon and arrange in a serving dish.

Bring the liquid in the pan to the boil and boil for 20 seconds until it is slightly thickened. Season the sauce to taste with salt and pepper.

Pass the sauce through a sieve to remove some of the seeds and pour over the vegetables. Serve the ratatouille hot or cold.

Tasty Tip

This dish would be perfect served as an accompaniment to a baked fish dish. It is also delicious in an omelette or as a jacket potato filling.

Creamy Vegetable Korma

Ingredients (Serves 4-6)

2 tbsp ghee or vegetable oil
1 large onion, peeled and chopped
2 garlic cloves, peeled and crushed
2.5 cm/1 in piece fresh root ginger, peeled and grated
4 cardamom pods
2 tsp ground coriander
1 tsp ground cumin
1 tsp ground turmeric
finely grated zest and juice of $\frac{1}{2}$ lemon
50 g/2 oz/$\frac{1}{2}$ cup ground almonds
400 ml/14 fl oz/1$\frac{2}{3}$ cups vegetable stock
450 g/1 lb potatoes, peeled and diced
450 g/1 lb mixed vegetables, such as cauliflower,
    carrots and turnip, cut into chunks
150 ml/$\frac{1}{4}$ pt/$\frac{2}{3}$ cup double/heavy cream
3 tbsp freshly chopped coriander/cilantro
salt and freshly ground black pepper
naan bread, to serve

Heat the ghee or oil in a large saucepan. Add the onion and cook for 5 minutes. Stir in the garlic and ginger and cook for a further 5 minutes, or until soft and beginning to colour.

Stir in the cardamom, ground coriander, cumin and turmeric. Continue cooking over a low heat for 1 minute, stirring.

Stir in the lemon rind and juice and almonds. Blend in the vegetable stock. Slowly bring to the boil, stirring occasionally.

Add the potatoes and vegetables. Bring back to the boil, then reduce the heat, cover and simmer for 35–40 minutes, or until the vegetables are just tender. Check after 25 minutes and add a little more stock if needed.

Slowly stir in the cream and chopped coriander. Season to taste with salt and pepper. Cook very gently until heated through, but do not boil. Serve immediately with naan bread.

Food Fact

Ghee is butter, clarified by gently heating until all the water has been evaporated and the milk solids separated from the pure fat, which can be used to cook at high temperatures without burning. You can buy butter-based ghee as well as a vegetarian version in specialist shops and Indian grocery stores.

Baby Roast Potato Salad

Ingredients (Serves 4)

350 g/12 oz small shallots
sea salt and freshly ground black pepper
900 g/2 lb small even-sized new potatoes
2 tbsp olive oil
2 medium courgettes/zucchini
2 sprigs fresh rosemary
175 g/6 oz/¹/₂ lb cherry tomatoes
150 ml/¹/₄ pt/²/₃ cup sour cream
2 tbsp freshly snipped chives
¹/₄ tsp paprika

Preheat the oven to 200°C/400°F/Gas Mark 6. Trim the shallots, but leave the skins on. Put in a saucepan of lightly salted boiling water with the potatoes and cook for 5 minutes; drain. Separate the shallots and plunge them into cold water for 1 minute.

Put the oil in a baking sheet lined with kitchen foil in a roasting tin and heat for a few minutes. Peel the skins off the shallots – they should now come away easily. Add to the baking sheet or roasting tin with the potatoes and toss in the oil to coat. Sprinkle with a little sea salt. Roast the potatoes and shallots in the preheated oven for 10 minutes.

Meanwhile, trim the courgettes, halve lengthways and cut into 5 cm/2 in chunks. Add to the baking sheet or roasting tin, toss to mix and cook for 5 minutes.

Pierce the tomato skins with a sharp knife. Add to the sheet or tin with the rosemary and cook for a further 5 minutes, or until all the vegetables are tender. Remove the rosemary and discard. Grind a little black pepper over the vegetables.

Spoon into a wide serving bowl. Mix together the sour cream and chives and drizzle over the vegetables just before serving.

Panzerotti

Ingredients (Makes 16)

450 g/1 lb/3½ cups high-gluten/strong white flour
pinch of salt
1 tsp easy-blend/instant yeast
2 tbsp olive oil
300 ml/½ pt/1¼ cups warm water
fresh rocket/arugula leaves, to serve

FOR THE FILLING:
1 tbsp olive oil
1 small red onion, peeled and finely chopped
2 garlic cloves, peeled and crushed
½ yellow pepper/bell pepper, deseeded and chopped
1 small courgette/zucchini, trimmed and chopped
50 g/2 oz/5 tbsp black olives, pitted and quartered
125 g/4 oz/1 cup mozzarella cheese, cut into
   tiny cubes
salt and freshly ground black pepper
5–6 tbsp tomato puree/paste
1 tsp dried mixed herbs
oil for deep-frying

Sift the flour and salt into a bowl. Stir in the yeast. Make a well in the centre. Add the oil and the warm water and mix to a soft dough. Knead on a lightly floured surface until smooth and elastic. Put in an oiled bowl, cover and leave in a warm place to rise while making the filling.

To make the filling, heat the oil in a frying pan and cook the onion for 5 minutes. Add the garlic, yellow pepper and courgette. Cook for about 5 minutes, or until the vegetables are tender. Tip into a bowl and leave to cool slightly. Stir in the olives and mozzarella cheese and season to taste with salt and pepper.

Briefly re-knead the dough. Divide into 16 equal pieces. Roll out each to a circle about 10 cm/4 in. Mix together the tomato puree and dried herbs, then spread about 1 teaspoon on each circle, leaving a 2 cm/¾ in border around the edge.

Divide the filling equally between the circles; it will seem a small amount but, if you overfill, they will leak during cooking. Brush the edges with water, then fold in half to enclose the filling. Press to seal, then crimp the edges.

Heat the oil in a deep-fat fryer to 180°C/350°F. Deep-fry the panzerotti in batches for 3 minutes, or until golden. Drain on absorbent kitchen paper and keep warm in a low oven until ready to serve with fresh rocket.

Courgette Lasagne

Ingredients (Serves 8)

2 tbsp olive oil
1 medium onion, peeled and finely chopped
225 g/8 oz/4 cups mushrooms, wiped and thinly sliced
3–4 courgettes/zucchini, trimmed and thinly sliced
2 garlic cloves, peeled and finely chopped
$^1/_2$ tsp dried thyme
1–2 tbsp freshly chopped basil or flat-leaf parsley
salt and freshly ground black pepper
1 quantity prepared white sauce (see page 140
350 g/12 oz lasagne sheets, cooked
225 g/8 oz/2 cups mozzarella cheese, grated
50 g/2 oz/$^1/_2$ cup Parmesan cheese, grated
400 g/14 oz can chopped tomatoes, drained

 Preheat the oven to 200°C/400°F/Gas Mark 6, 15 minutes before cooking. Heat the oil in a large frying pan, add the onion and cook for 3–5 minutes. Add the mushrooms, cook for 2 minutes, then add the courgettes and cook for a further 3–4 minutes, or until tender. Stir in the garlic, thyme and basil or parsley and season to taste with salt and pepper. Remove from the heat and reserve.

 Spoon one-third of the white sauce on to the base of a lightly oiled large baking dish. Arrange a layer of lasagne over the sauce. Spread half the courgette mixture over the pasta, then sprinkle with some of the mozzarella and some of the Parmesan cheese. Repeat with more white sauce and another layer of lasagne, then cover with half the drained tomatoes.

 Cover the tomatoes with lasagne, the remaining courgette mixture and some mozzarella and Parmesan cheese. Repeat the layers, ending with a layer of lasagne sheets, white sauce and the remaining Parmesan cheese. Bake in the preheated oven for 35 minutes, or until golden. Serve immediately.

Roasted Vegetable Pie

Ingredients (Serves 4)

225 g/8 oz/1¾ cups plain/all-purpose flour
pinch of salt
50 g/2 oz/4 tbsp white vegetable fat, lard or
 shortening, cut into squares
50 g/2 oz/4 tbsp butter, cut into squares
2 tsp herbes de Provence
1 red pepper/bell pepper, deseeded and halved
1 green pepper/bell pepper, deseeded and halved
1 yellow pepper/bell pepper, deseeded and halved
3 tbsp extra virgin olive oil
1 aubergine/eggplant, trimmed and sliced
1 courgette/zucchini, trimmed and halved lengthways
1 leek, trimmed and cut into chunks
1 medium/large egg, beaten
125 g/4 oz/1 cup fresh mozzarella cheese, sliced
salt and freshly ground black pepper
sprigs of mixed herbs, to garnish

Preheat the oven to 220°C/425°F/Gas Mark 7. Sift the flour and salt into a large bowl, add the fats and mix lightly. Rub together until it resembles breadcrumbs. Stir in the herbes de Provence. Sprinkle over a tablespoon of cold water and, with a knife, start bringing the dough together. (It may be necessary to use your hands for the final stage.) If it does not form a ball instantly, add a little more water. Place in a polythene bag and chill for 30 minutes.

Place the peppers on a baking tray and sprinkle with 1 tablespoon of the oil. Roast in the oven for 20 minutes, or until the skins start to blacken. Brush the aubergines, courgettes and leeks with oil and place on another baking tray. Roast with the peppers for 20 minutes. Place the peppers in a polythene bag and leave the skin to loosen for 5 minutes. When cool enough to handle, peel the skins off the peppers.

 Roll out half the pastry on a lightly floured surface and use to line a 20.5 cm/8 in round pie dish. Line the pastry with greaseproof paper and fill with baking beans or rice and bake blind for about 10 minutes. Remove the beans and the paper, then brush the base with a little of the beaten egg. Return to the oven for 5 minutes.

Layer the cooked vegetables and the cheese in the pastry case, seasoning each layer. Roll out the remaining pastry and cut out the lid 5 mm/¼ in wider than the dish. Brush the rim with some beaten egg and lay the lid on top, then press to seal. Knock the edges with the back of a knife. Cut a slit in the lid and brush with egg. Bake for 30 minutes. Garnish with sprigs of herbs and serve immediately.

Marinated Vegetable Kebabs

Ingredients (Serves 4)

2 small courgettes/zucchini, cut into 2 cm/^{3}/$_4$ in pieces
^{1}/$_2$ green pepper/bell pepper, deseeded
    and cut into 2.5 cm/1 in pieces
^{1}/$_2$ red pepper/bell pepper, deseeded
    and cut into 2.5 cm /1 in pieces
^{1}/$_2$ yellow pepper/bell pepper, deseeded
    and cut into 2.5 cm/1 in pieces
8 baby onions, peeled
8 button mushrooms
8 cherry tomatoes
freshly chopped parsley, to garnish
freshly cooked couscous, to serve

FOR THE MARINADE:
1 tbsp light olive oil
4 tbsp dry sherry
2 tbsp light soy sauce
1 red chilli, deseeded and finely chopped
2 garlic cloves, peeled and crushed
2.5 cm/1 in piece root ginger, peeled and finely grated

 Place the courgettes, peppers and baby onions in a pan of just-boiled water. Bring back to the boil and simmer for about 30 seconds, then drain and rinse the cooked vegetables in cold water and dry on absorbent kitchen paper.

Thread the cooked vegetables and the mushrooms and tomatoes alternately on to skewers and place in a large shallow dish.

Make the marinade by whisking all the ingredients together until thoroughly blended. Pour the marinade evenly over the kebabs, then chill in the refrigerator for at least 1 hour. Spoon the marinade over the kebabs occasionally during this time.

Place the kebabs in a hot griddle pan or on a hot barbecue and cook gently for 10–12 minutes. Turn the kebabs frequently and brush with the marinade when needed. When the vegetables are tender, sprinkle over the chopped parsley and serve immediately with couscous.

Tasty Tip

If using wooden skewers and cooking over a barbecue, soak in cold water for 30 minutes before using. Although these kebabs use only vegetables, large chunks of fish, such as cod, or indeed tiger prawns/jumbo shrimp could be added alternately between the vegetables and cooked as in step 4.

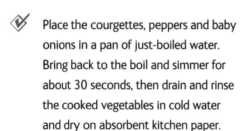

Chargrilled Vegetable and Goats' Cheese Pizza

Ingredients (Serves 4)

125 g/4 oz baking potato
1 tbsp olive oil
225 g/8 oz/1¼ cups strong white bread flour
½ tsp salt
1 tsp easy-blend/instant yeast

FOR THE TOPPING:
1 medium aubergine/eggplant, thinly sliced
2 small courgettes/zucchini, trimmed and
   sliced lengthways
1 yellow pepper/bell pepper, quartered and deseeded
1 red onion, peeled and sliced into very thin wedges
5 tbsp olive oil
175 g/6 oz/1½ cups cooked new potatoes, halved
400 g/14 oz can chopped tomatoes, drained
2 tsp freshly chopped oregano
125 g/4 oz/⅓ cup mozzarella cheese,
   cut into small cubes
125 g/4 oz/⅓ cup goats' cheese, crumbled

 Preheat the oven to 220°C/425°F/Gas Mark 7, 15 minutes before baking. Put a baking sheet in the oven to heat up. Cook the potato in lightly salted boiling water until tender. Peel and mash with the olive oil until smooth.

 Sift the flour and salt into a bowl. Stir in the yeast. Add the mashed potato and 150 ml/¼ pt/⅔ cup warm water and mix to a soft dough. Knead for 5–6 minutes until smooth. Put the dough in a bowl, cover with clingfilm/plastic wrap and leave to rise in a warm place for 30 minutes.

 To make the topping, arrange the aubergine, courgettes, pepper and onion, skin-side up, on a grill/broiler rack and brush with 4 tablespoons of the oil. Grill for 4–5 minutes. Turn the vegetables and brush with the remaining oil. Grill for 3–4 minutes. Cool, skin and slice the pepper. Put the vegetables in a bowl, add the halved new potatoes and gently toss together. Set aside.

Briefly re-knead the dough, then roll out to a 30.5–35.5 cm/12–14 in round, according to preferred thickness. Mix the tomatoes and oregano together and spread over the base. Scatter over the mozzarella. Put the pizza on the preheated baking sheet and bake for 8 minutes. Arrange the vegetables and goats' cheese on top and bake for 8–10 minutes. Serve.

Pumpkin-filled Pasta with Butter and Sage

Ingredients (Serves 6-8)

FOR THE PASTA DOUGH:
225 g/8 oz/1¼ cups strong plain bread flour or
 type 00 pasta flour, plus extra for rolling
1 tsp salt
2 medium/large eggs
1 medium/large egg yolk
1 tbsp extra virgin olive oil

FOR THE FILLING:
250 g/9 oz/1 cup freshly cooked pumpkin or
 sweet potato flesh, mashed and cooled
75–125 g/3–4 oz/⅓ cup dried breadcrumbs
125 g/4 oz/1 cup freshly grated Parmesan cheese
1 medium/large egg yolk
½ tsp soft brown sugar
2 tbsp freshly chopped parsley
freshly grated nutmeg
salt and freshly ground black pepper
125 g/4 oz/1 stick butter
2 tbsp freshly shredded sage leaves
50 g/2 oz/½ cup freshly grated Parmesan
 cheese, to serve

 To make the dough, sift the flour and salt into a large bowl, make a well in the centre and add the eggs, egg yolk, oil and 1 teaspoon water. Gradually mix to form a soft but not sticky dough, adding a little more flour or water as necessary. Turn out on to a lightly floured surface and knead for 5 minutes, or until smooth and elastic. Wrap in clingfilm/plastic wrap and leave to rest at room temperature for about 30 minutes.

 Mix together the ingredients for the filling in a bowl, seasoning to taste with freshly grated nutmeg, salt and pepper. If the mixture seems too wet, add a few more breadcrumbs to bind.

Cut the pasta dough into quarters. Work with one quarter at a time, covering the remaining quarters with a damp tea towel. Roll out a quarter very thinly into a strip 10 cm/4 in wide. Drop spoonfuls of the filling along the strip 6.5 cm/2½ in apart, in 2 rows about 5 cm/2 in apart. Moisten the outside edges and the spaces between the filling with water.

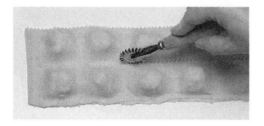

 Roll out another strip of pasta and lay it over the filled strip. Press down gently along both edges and between the filled sections. Using a fluted pastry wheel, cut along both long sides, down the centre and between the fillings to form cushions. Transfer the cushions to a lightly floured baking sheet. Continue making cushions and allow to dry for 30 minutes.

Bring a large saucepan of slightly salted water to the boil. Add the pasta cushions and return to the boil. Cook, stirring frequently, for 4–5 minutes, or until *al dente*. Drain carefully.

Heat the butter in a pan, stir in the shredded sage leaves and cook for 30 seconds. Add the pasta cushions, stir gently, then spoon into serving bowls. Sprinkle with the grated Parmesan cheese and serve immediately.

Budget Tip

Making your own pasta from scratch can save you money by buying the cheap, raw ingredients in bulk. You not only know what goes into it, but you can always freeze what you do not use for another time (if you freeze whole lumps of dough, make sure you take them out the day before in order to defrost thoroughly).

Rice with Squash and Sage

Ingredients (Serves 4-6)

450 g/1 lb butternut squash
75 g/3 oz/²/₃ stick unsalted butter
1 small onion, peeled and finely chopped
3 garlic cloves, peeled and crushed
2 tbsp freshly chopped sage
1 l/1³/₄ pts/4 cups vegetable or chicken stock
450 g/1 lb Arborio/risotto rice
50 g/2 oz/¹/₂ cup pine nuts, toasted
25 g/1 oz/¹/₄ cup freshly grated Parmesan cheese
freshly snipped chives, to garnish
salt and freshly ground black pepper

Peel the squash, cut in half lengthways and remove seeds and stringy flesh. Cut the remaining flesh into small cubes and reserve.

Heat the wok, add the butter and heat until foaming, then add the

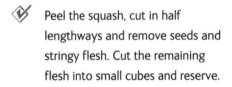

onion, garlic and sage and stir-fry for 1 minute.

Add the squash to the wok and stir-fry for an additional 10–12 minutes, or until the squash is tender. Remove from the heat.

Meanwhile, bring the vegetable or chicken stock to the boil and add the rice. Cook for 8–10 minutes, or until the rice is just tender but still quite wet.

Add the cooked rice to the squash mixture. Stir in the pine nuts and Parmesan, season to taste with salt and pepper. Garnish with snipped chives and serve immediately.

Corn Fritters with Hot and Spicy Relish

Ingredients (Makes 16-20)

325 g/11 oz can sweetcorn kernels, drained
1 onion, peeled and very finely chopped
1 spring onion/scallion, trimmed and
   very finely chopped
¹/₂ tsp chilli powder
1 tsp ground coriander
4 tbsp plain/all-purpose flour
1 tsp baking powder
1 medium/large egg
salt and freshly ground black pepper
300 ml/¹/₂ pt/1¹/₄ cups groundnut/peanut oil
sprigs of fresh coriander/cilantro, to garnish

FOR THE SPICY RELISH:
3 tbsp sunflower oil
1 onion, peeled and very finely chopped
¹/₄ tsp dried crushed chillies
2 garlic cloves, peeled and crushed
2 tbsp plum sauce

 Make the relish. Heat a wok, add the sunflower oil and, when hot, add the onion and stir-fry for 3–4 minutes, or until softened. Add the chillies and garlic, stir-fry for 1 minute, then leave to cool slightly. Stir in the plum sauce, transfer to a food processor and blend until the consistency of chutney. Reserve.

Place the sweetcorn into a food processor and blend briefly until just mashed. Transfer to a bowl with the onions, chilli powder, coriander, flour, baking powder and egg. Season to taste with salt and pepper and mix together.

 Heat a wok, add the oil and heat to 180˚C/350˚F. Working in batches, drop a few spoonfuls of the sweetcorn mixture into the oil and deep-fry for 3–4 minutes, or until golden and crispy, turning occasionally. Using a slotted spoon, remove and drain on absorbent kitchen paper. Arrange on a warmed serving platter, garnish with sprigs of coriander and serve immediately with the relish.

Crispy Pancake Rolls

Ingredients (Makes 8)

250 g/9 oz/2 cups plain/all-purpose flour
pinch of salt
1 medium/large egg
4 tsp sunflower oil
2 tbsp light olive oil
2 cm/³/₄ in piece fresh root ginger, peeled and grated
1 garlic clove, peeled and crushed
225 g/8 oz/¹/₂ lb tofu, drained and cut into small dice
2 tbsp soy sauce
1 tbsp dry sherry
175 g/6 oz/1¹/₂ cups button mushrooms,
   wiped and chopped
1 celery stalk, trimmed and finely chopped
2 spring onions/scallions, trimmed and finely chopped
2 tbsp groundnut/peanut oil
fresh coriander/cilantro sprig and sliced spring
   onion/scallion, to garnish

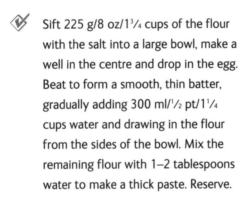

Sift 225 g/8 oz/1³/₄ cups of the flour with the salt into a large bowl, make a well in the centre and drop in the egg. Beat to form a smooth, thin batter, gradually adding 300 ml/¹/₂ pt/1¹/₄ cups water and drawing in the flour from the sides of the bowl. Mix the remaining flour with 1–2 tablespoons water to make a thick paste. Reserve.

Heat a little sunflower oil in a 20.5 cm /8 in omelette or frying pan and pour in 2 tablespoons of the batter. Cook for 1–2 minutes, flip over and cook for a further 1–2 minutes, or until

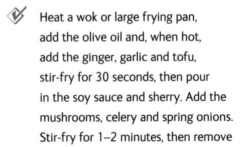

firm. Slide from the pan and keep warm. Make more pancakes with the remaining batter.

Heat a wok or large frying pan, add the olive oil and, when hot, add the ginger, garlic and tofu, stir-fry for 30 seconds, then pour in the soy sauce and sherry. Add the mushrooms, celery and spring onions. Stir-fry for 1–2 minutes, then remove from the wok and leave to cool.

Place a little filling in the centre of each pancake. Brush the edges with the flour paste, fold in the edges, then roll up into parcels. Heat the groundnut oil to 180˚C/350˚F in the wok. Fry the pancake rolls for 2–3 minutes, or until golden. Serve immediately, garnished with chopped spring onions and a sprig of coriander.

Creamy Chickpea Curry

Ingredients (Serves 4-6)

2 tbsp vegetable oil
1 cinnamon stick, bruised
3 cardamom pods, bruised
1 tsp fennel seeds
5 cm/2 in piece fresh root ginger, peeled and grated
2 garlic cloves, peeled and crushed
2 red chillies, deseeded and chopped
1 large onion, peeled and chopped
1 tsp ground fenugreek
1 tsp garam masala
$^{1}/_{2}$ tsp turmeric
2 x 400 g/14 oz cans chickpeas, drained and rinsed
300 ml/$^{1}/_{2}$ pt/1$^{1}/_{4}$ cups water
1 tsp tomato puree/paste
300 ml/$^{1}/_{2}$ pt/1$^{1}/_{4}$ cups coconut milk
225 g/8 oz/$^{1}/_{2}$ cup cherry tomatoes, halved
2 tbsp freshly chopped coriander/cilantro

 Heat the oil in a frying pan, add the cinnamon stick, cardamom pods, fennel seeds and ginger and cook gently for 3 minutes, stirring frequently. Add the garlic, chillies, onion and remaining spices to the pan and cook gently, stirring occasionally, for 3–5 minutes, or until the onion has softened.

Add the chickpeas and water. Bring to the boil, then reduce the heat and simmer for 15 minutes.

Blend the tomato puree with a little of the coconut milk, then add to the chickpeas with the remaining coconut milk and tomatoes. Cook for 8–10 minutes, or until the tomatoes have begun to collapse. Stir in the chopped coriander and serve.

Helpful hint
Medium-sized tomatoes can be used, if preferred – simply chop rather than halve and use as above.

Recipes: Desserts & Sweet Treats

PACKED WITH • MONEY SAVING • IDEAS & TIPS

Rice Pudding

Ingredients (Serves 4)

60 g/2½ oz/¾ cup pudding rice
50 g/2 oz/¼ cup granulated sugar
410 g/14 oz can evaporated milk
300 ml/½ pt/1¼ cups milk
pinch of freshly grated nutmeg
25 g/1 oz/¼ stick butter or margarine
jam/jelly, to decorate

Preheat the oven to 150°C/300°F/Gas Mark 2. Lightly oil a large ovenproof dish.

Sprinkle the rice and the sugar into the dish and mix.

Bring the evaporated milk and milk to the boil in a small pan, stirring occasionally.

Stir the milks into the rice and mix well until the rice is coated thoroughly.

Sprinkle over the nutmeg, cover with kitchen foil and bake in the preheated oven for 30 minutes.

Remove the pudding from the oven and stir well, breaking up any lumps.

Cover with the same kitchen foil. Bake in the preheated oven for a further 30 minutes. Remove from the oven and stir well again.

Dot the pudding with butter and bake for a further 45–60 minutes, until the rice is tender and the skin is browned.

Divide the pudding into four individual serving bowls. Top with a large spoonful of the jam and serve immediately.

Tasty Tip

The main trick to achieving traditional creamy rice pudding is not using cream and full-fat milk (you can use light or low-fat milks and butter in this recipe), but instead long, slow cooking on a low temperature. Try adding a few sultanas and lemon peel, or a few roughly crushed cardamom pods for an alternative flavour.

Oaty Fruit Puddings

Ingredients (Serves 4)

125 g/4 oz/1¼ cups rolled oats/oatmeal
50 g/2 oz/¼ cup butter or margarine, melted
2 tbsp chopped almonds
1 tbsp clear honey
pinch of ground cinnamon
2 pears, peeled, cored and finely chopped
1 tbsp marmalade
orange zest, to decorate
custard or fruit-flavoured yoghurt, to serve

Preheat the oven to 200°C/400°F/Gas Mark 6. Lightly oil and line the bases of four individual pudding bowls or muffin tins with a small circle of greaseproof paper.

Mix together the oats, butter, nuts, honey and cinnamon in a small bowl.

Using a spoon, spread two thirds of the oaty mixture over the base and around the sides of the pudding bowls or muffin tins.

Toss together the pears and marmalade and spoon into the oaty cases.

Scatter over the remaining oaty mixture to cover the pears and marmalade.

Bake in the preheated oven for 15–20 minutes, until cooked and the tops of the puddings are golden and crisp.

Leave for 5 minutes before removing the pudding bowls or the muffin tins. Decorate with orange zest and serve hot with custard or fruit-flavoured yoghurt.

Tasty Tip

For the older members of the family, liqueur custard is superb with steamed and baked puddings. Add 2–3 table-spoons of either Cointreau or a liqueur of your choice to the custard, together with 1 teaspoon of vanilla essence. Taste the custard and add more alcohol if desired.

Summer Pavlova

Ingredients (Serves 6-8)

4 medium/large egg whites
225 g/8 oz/1 cup caster/superfine sugar
1 tsp vanilla essence
2 tsp white wine vinegar
1½ tsp cornflour/cornstarch
300 ml/½ pt/1 cup half-fat Greek-set/plain yoghurt
2 tbsp honey
225 g/8 oz/2 cups strawberries, hulled
125 g/4 oz/1 cup raspberries
125 g/4 oz/1 cup blueberries
4 kiwis, peeled and sliced
icing/confectioners' sugar, to decorate

 Preheat the oven to 150°C/300°F/Gas Mark 2. Line a baking sheet with a sheet of greaseproof paper or baking parchment.

 Place the egg whites in a clean grease-free bowl and whisk until very stiff. Whisk in half the sugar, vanilla essence, vinegar and cornflour; continue whisking until stiff. Gradually whisk in the remaining sugar, a teaspoonful at a time, until very stiff and glossy.

 Using a large spoon, arrange spoonfuls of the meringue in a circle on the greaseproof paper or baking parchment. Bake in the preheated oven for 1 hour until crisp and dry. Turn the oven off and leave the meringue in the oven to cool completely.

 Remove the meringue from the baking sheet and peel away the parchment. Mix together the yoghurt and honey. Place the pavlova on a serving plate and spoon the yoghurt into the centre. Scatter over the strawberries, raspberries, blueberries and kiwis. Dust with the icing sugar and serve.

Helpful Hint
Any grease in the bowl will prevent the egg whites from rising into the stiff consistency necessary for this recipe.

Raspberry Sorbet Crush

Ingredients (Serves 4)

225 g/8 oz/2 cups raspberries, thawed if frozen
zest and juice of 1 lime
300 ml/½ pt/1¼ cups orange juice
225 g/8 oz/1 cup caster/superfine sugar
2 medium/large egg whites

Set the freezer to rapid freeze. If using fresh raspberries, pick over and lightly rinse. Place the raspberries in a dish and, using a masher, mash to a chunky puree.

Place the lime zest and juice, orange juice and half the caster sugar in a large, heavy-based saucepan. Heat gently, stirring frequently until the sugar is dissolved. Bring to the boil and boil rapidly for about 5 minutes. Remove the pan from the heat and pour carefully into a freezable container. Leave to cool, then place in the freezer and freeze for 2 hours, stirring occasionally to break up the ice crystals.

Fold the ice mixture into the raspberry puree with a metal spoon and freeze for a further 2 hours, stirring occasionally.

Whisk the egg whites until stiff, then gradually whisk in the remaining caster sugar a tablespoon at a time until the egg white mixture is stiff and glossy. Fold into the raspberry sorbet with a metal spoon and freeze for 1 hour. Spoon into tall glasses and serve immediately. Remember to return the freezer to its normal setting.

Food Fact
This recipe contains raw egg and so should not be given to babies, young children, pregnant women, the sick, the elderly or those suffering from a recurring illness.

Chocolate Chip Cookies

Ingredients (Makes about 30)

140 g/4½ oz/1 stick butter
50 g/2 oz/¼ cup caster/superfine sugar
60 g/2½ oz/⅓ cup soft dark brown sugar
1 medium/large egg, beaten
½ tsp vanilla essence
125 g/4 oz/½ cup plain/all-purpose flour
½ tsp bicarbonate of soda
150 g/5 oz/¾ cup plain or milk chocolate chips

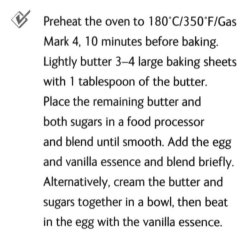

Preheat the oven to 180°C/350°F/Gas Mark 4, 10 minutes before baking. Lightly butter 3–4 large baking sheets with 1 tablespoon of the butter. Place the remaining butter and both sugars in a food processor and blend until smooth. Add the egg and vanilla essence and blend briefly. Alternatively, cream the butter and sugars together in a bowl, then beat in the egg with the vanilla essence.

If using a food processor, scrape out the mixture with a spatula and place it into a large bowl. Sift the flour and bicarbonate of soda together, then fold into the creamed mixture. When the mixture is blended thoroughly, stir in the chocolate chips.

Drop heaped teaspoons of the mixture on to the prepared baking sheets, spaced well apart, and bake the cookies in the preheated oven for 10–12 minutes, or until lightly golden.

Leave to cool for a few seconds, then, using a spatula, transfer to a wire rack and cool completely. The cookies are best eaten when just cooked, but can be stored in an airtight tin for a few days.

Helpful Hint

For light-textured, crumbly cookies, do not overwork the dough. Handle as little as possible and fold the ingredients together gently in a figure of 8 using a metal spoon or rubber spatula. To ring the changes with these basic biscuits, use an equal mixture of chocolate chips and nuts. Alternatively, replace the chocolate chips entirely with an equal quantity of your favourite chopped nuts.

Lemon Bars

Ingredients (Makes 24)

175 g/6 oz/1⅓ cups, plus 2 tbsp, plain/all-purpose flour
125 g/4 oz/1 stick butter
50 g/2 oz/¼ cup granulated sugar
200 g/7 oz/1 cup caster/superfine sugar
½ tsp baking powder
¼ tsp salt
2 medium/large eggs, lightly beaten
juice and finely grated zest of 1 lemon
sifted icing/confectioners' sugar, to decorate

Preheat the oven to 170°C/325°F/Gas Mark 3, 10 minutes before baking. Lightly oil and line a 20.5 cm/8 in square cake tin with greaseproof or baking paper.

Rub together the flour, reserving the 2 tablespoons' worth, and butter until the mixture resembles breadcrumbs. Stir in the granulated sugar and mix. Turn the mixture into the prepared tin and press down firmly. Bake in the preheated oven for 20 minutes, until a pale golden colour.

Meanwhile, in a food processor, mix together the caster sugar, remaining flour, baking powder, salt, eggs, lemon juice and zest until smooth. Pour over the prepared base.

Transfer to the preheated oven and bake for a further 20–25 minutes, until nearly set but still a bit wobbly in the centre. Remove from the oven and cool in the tin on a wire rack.

Dust with icing sugar and cut into squares. Serve cold or store in an airtight tin.

Food Fact

Baking powder is a chemically prepared raising agent consisting of cream of tartar and bicarbonate of soda, which is then mixed with a dried starch or flour. It is very important to measure accurately, otherwise the mixture could either not rise, or rise too quickly and then collapse, and give a sour taste to the dish.

Peach and Chocolate Bake

Ingredients (Serves 6)

200 g/7 oz plain dark chocolate
125 g/4 oz/½ cup unsalted butter
4 medium/large eggs, separated
125 g/4 oz/1¼ cups caster/superfine sugar
425 g/15 oz can peach slices, drained
½ tsp ground cinnamon
1 tbsp icing/confectioners' sugar, sifted, to decorate
crème fraîche, to serve

Preheat the oven to 170°C/325°F/Gas Mark 3, 10 minutes before baking. Lightly oil a 1.7 l/3 pt ovenproof dish.

Break the chocolate and butter into small pieces and place in a small heat-proof bowl set over a saucepan of gently simmering water. Ensure water is not touching the base of the bowl and leave to melt. Remove the bowl from the heat and stir until smooth.

Whisk the egg yolks with the sugar until very thick and creamy, then stir the melted chocolate and butter into the whisked egg yolk mixture and mix together lightly.

Place the egg whites in a clean, grease-free bowl and whisk until stiff, then fold 2 tablespoons of the whisked egg whites into the chocolate mixture. Mix well, then add the remaining egg white and fold in very lightly.

Fold the peach slices and the cinnamon into the mixture, then spoon the mixture into the prepared dish. Do not level the mixture, leave a little uneven.

Bake in the preheated oven for 35–40 minutes, or until well risen and just firm to the touch. Sprinkle the bake with the icing sugar and serve immediately with spoonfuls of crème fraîche.

Queen of Puddings

Ingredients (Serves 4)

75 g/3 oz/³⁄₄ cup fresh white breadcrumbs
25 g/1 oz/¹⁄₈ cup granulated sugar
450 ml/³⁄₄ pt/1³⁄₄ cups whole milk
25 g/1 oz/¹⁄₄ stick butter
grated zest of 1 small lemon
2 medium/large eggs, separated
2 tbsp seedless raspberry jam/jelly
50 g/2 oz/¹⁄₄ cup caster/superfine sugar

Preheat the oven to 170°C/325°F/Gas Mark 3. Oil a 900 ml/1¹⁄₂ pt ovenproof baking dish and reserve.

Mix the breadcrumbs and sugar together in a bowl.

Pour the milk into a small saucepan and heat gently with the butter and lemon zest until the butter has melted.

Allow the mixture to cool a little, then pour over the breadcrumbs. Stir well and leave to soak for 30 minutes.

Whisk the egg yolks into the cooled breadcrumb mixture and pour into the prepared dish.

Place the dish on a baking sheet and bake in the preheated oven for about 30 minutes, or until firm and set. Remove from the oven.

Allow to cool slightly, then spread the jam over the pudding. Whisk the egg whites until stiff and standing in peaks.

Gently fold in the caster sugar with a metal spoon or rubber spatula. Pile the meringue over the top of the pudding.

Return the dish to the oven for a further 25–30 minutes, or until the meringue is crisp and just slightly coloured. Serve hot or cold.

Rich Double-crust Plum Pie

Ingredients (Serves 6)

FOR THE PASTRY:
75 g/3 oz/²/₃ stick butter
75 g/3 oz/¹/₃ cup white vegetable fat
225 g/8 oz/1¾ cups plain/all-purpose flour
2 medium/large egg yolks

FOR THE FILLING:
450 g/1 lb fresh plums, preferably Victoria
50 g/2 oz/¼ cup caster/superfine sugar
1 tbsp milk
a little extra caster/superfine sugar, to decorate

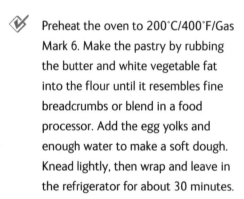

Preheat the oven to 200°C/400°F/Gas Mark 6. Make the pastry by rubbing the butter and white vegetable fat into the flour until it resembles fine breadcrumbs or blend in a food processor. Add the egg yolks and enough water to make a soft dough. Knead lightly, then wrap and leave in the refrigerator for about 30 minutes.

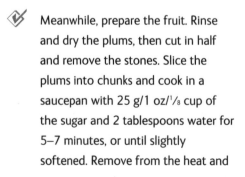

Meanwhile, prepare the fruit. Rinse and dry the plums, then cut in half and remove the stones. Slice the plums into chunks and cook in a saucepan with 25 g/1 oz/¹/₈ cup of the sugar and 2 tablespoons water for 5–7 minutes, or until slightly softened. Remove from the heat and add the remaining sugar to taste and allow to cool.

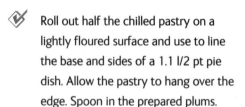

Roll out half the chilled pastry on a lightly floured surface and use to line the base and sides of a 1.1 l/2 pt pie dish. Allow the pastry to hang over the edge. Spoon in the prepared plums.

Roll out the remaining pastry to use as the lid and brush the edge with a little water. Wrap the pastry around the rolling pin and place over the plums. Press the edges together to seal and mark a decorative edge around the rim of the pastry by pinching with the thumb and forefinger or using the back of a fork. Brush the lid with milk and make a few slits in the top. Use any trimmings to decorate the top of the pie with pastry leaves. Place on a baking sheet and bake in the preheated oven for 30 minutes, or until golden brown. Sprinkle with a little caster sugar and serve hot or cold.